Snapshots

of *the*

Kingdom

Snapshots

of the

Kingdom

Glimpses of Heaven on Earth

Steve Rodeheaver

Beacon Hill Press of Kansas City
Kansas City, Missouri

Copyright 1998
by Beacon Hill Press of Kansas City

ISBN 083-411-7061

Printed in the
United States of America

Cover Design: Kevin Williamson

Library of Congress Cataloging-in-Publication Data
Rodeheaver, Steve, 1961-
     Snapshots of the Kingdom / Steve Rodeheaver.
        p.   cm.
     ISBN 0-8341-1706-1
     1. Kingdom of God. 2. Church work with the poor. I. Title.
BT94.R54   1998
253—dc21   97-47388
                                            CIP

10   9   8   7   6   5   4   3   2   1

To
My wife, Vonda
My children, Rebecca, Rachel, and John Mark
and my Kingdom brothers and sisters
at
San Diego, Calif.,
Southeast Church of the Nazarene

Contents

INTRODUCTION

"SHOULD I GET SLIDES OR PRINTS?" I asked Vonda, my wife, as I was about to go buy some film. She answered as if it wasn't a question, "Get prints. We'll look at them more, they are easier to show friends and family, and we can get an extra set free to give to relatives." We have three children, two daughters and one son, and lots of relatives who live out of state, including Vonda's parents, who live in Michigan. I picked up a bulk package of six rolls of print film.

On my desk I have a snapshot of my wife and me from the first time I brought her to San Diego to meet my folks. On the lampstand there are snapshots of our older daughter, Rebecca, when she was six months old and our younger daughter, Rachel, when she was nine months old. On the walls of my home office are pictures of my parents, brothers, and best friends from college days. On the refrigerator are wallet-size pictures of our friends' children. Throughout the house, in just about every room, are photographs of our immediate family, grandparents, uncles, aunts, and some folks that I don't know much about except that I'm related to them. We don't have enough wall space or frames to hang all the snapshots that we've collected over the years. We have drawers and photo albums full of snapshots. We like to get them out and look at them from time to time.

Why all the snapshots? Why so many photographs? Because they help us remember, especially times and places important to us. They remind us of people and relationships and priorities. They help us remember who we are. They define us.

This remembering is not as my computer remembers. It is not just a recalling of facts and data. Rather, snapshots help us to reexperience the moment captured. Feelings and emotions are re-created. The story of the picture is relived. We make contact with the past. The snapshot is more than a pose. It is a piece of the past that, when looked at and remembered, actually brings the past into the present.

Have you ever thought of the Gospels as snapshots of Jesus' life and ministry? Each episode, each story, is a verbal snapshot of Jesus. By looking at them over the centuries, the Church has remembered who Jesus is and what He is about. These snapshots have served to define not only Christ but also His followers. We encounter Jesus in these memories of Him. The past becomes present, and we are challenged to follow Jesus, just as those first disciples were challenged. Like snapshots of our families, they are defining moments for us.

There is something very unique about snapshots of Jesus. Not only are they snapshots of the *past*, but also they are snapshots of the *future*. Jesus preached that the kingdom of God was at hand. In fact, it was present in our Lord himself. Jesus' teaching, preaching, and ministry were snapshots of what that Kingdom is like. But while Jesus talked about the presence of the Kingdom and called men to enter into it by following Him, He also taught that the Kingdom would not come in its fullness until He himself returned. Thus, in Jesus and His disciples the Kingdom was present—but only in a snapshot sort of way. The fullness of the Kingdom was yet to come. In short, Jesus came to us bringing pictures of the future. As we are encountered by these snapshots, we are called to enter into the Kingdom, to live in the future and have the future live in us. We enter the Kingdom by following Jesus. We receive His Spirit as we come to Him. As we follow Him and allow Him to rule and direct our lives, we, too, become snapshots of the Kingdom.

I am convinced that one of the primary purposes of the Church, of the community of followers of Jesus, is to be a snapshot of the Kingdom. When folks look at the Church, they should get a glimpse of the Kingdom. When people see you and me following Jesus, they should see wallet-size pictures of the coming Kingdom. Jesus brought the future rule of God into the present. If Christ is reigning in us, then the future is present as well. We are snapshots of the coming Kingdom. By looking at and considering us, folks will be able to remember and experience the future that God is coming. They, too, will be called to enter into the Kingdom.

The chapters that follow are snapshots of the Kingdom. Most of them are taken from the church I'm privileged to pastor in San Diego. God has blessed me by surrounding me with many living pictures of His saving work. While His work is not yet complete, and sometimes I'm tempted to give up, I have snapshots that prove His kingdom is coming. Those snapshots keep me living toward the future. I hope they encourage you as well to keep on seeking first the Kingdom.

Just a couple of notes before getting started. In the pictures that follow, some of the names and details have been changed to protect identities. Also, this "scroll" of film has taken roughly three years to develop. The pictures span close to eight years of ministry. Given that life is full of changes, it goes without saying that some of the pictures are not up-to-date. They, nonetheless, serve as exposures of the Kingdom.

EXPOSURE 1:

And They Were All Satisfied

$\mathcal{I}$T WAS WEDNESDAY AFTERNOON, and I was starting to get nervous. In just a few hours we would be serving our fourth annual Thanksgiving Eve dinner. The church had really pulled together in planning and preparing this dinner. It's one of our most meaningful ways of reaching out to our neighborhood and showing the love of Christ. Everyone is invited. There's no required sermon to sit through. No ID is needed. It does not matter what your reason is for coming, you are welcome.

We serve the dinner in the sanctuary. Our sanctuary does not have pews. Instead, we have stacking chairs. This allows us to do more with our limited space. We had set up tables and chairs to seat about 100. Red-and-white-checkered tablecloths gave the church a very homey feeling. All the places were set. There were autumn centerpieces on each table. Everything looked great!

I was in the kitchen, and, as I was saying, I was getting a little nervous and starting to worry. What if we prepared this huge feast and nobody came? Or what if after spreading the word about this fantastic meal, we ran out of food? Our first Thanksgiving Eve dinner we served about 100 people, our second Thanksgiving about 150, and last year we served nearly 200. This year we were planning on 200-250. We fixed 120 pounds of turkey (six 20-pound birds). We had pans and pans of dressing and yams and green beans and bread pudding. There was cranberry sauce and rolls. And to top it all off, we had what looked to be an unending supply of pumpkin and sweet potato pies. The ladies of the church had outdone themselves in preparing this dinner. I wish you could have been there just to smell the food. It was mouthwatering!

But what if nobody came? What if we planned and fixed all this food and nobody came? We had put the word out that we were serving the dinner. Lots of people said they were coming. But still, you never know. Or what if they all came? What if we ran out of food in 20 minutes? What if we had to turn away family after family because we didn't plan right?

I knew one person was coming for sure. We had invited our church district superintendent, Rev. Maurice Hall, to help serve the meal. He said he was looking forward to being with us. We learned that he even changed some family plans in order to join us. What if after he went to all the effort of changing holiday plans and traveling two hours to help serve this dinner, no one showed up? Then I would be the turkey. I was worried.

Well, 5:30 rolled around, and Rev. Hall arrived. But I was beginning to relax. Serving time wasn't until 6:00, and people were already starting to come in. By 6:00 all the seats were full, and more folks were outside. There were families of all sizes, colors, and backgrounds. There were grandmothers and babies and every age in between. There were homeless and poor. There were folks who had material possessions but were lonely. There were many who wanted to help. And all were thankful.

For the next hour and a half we visited, served, cleaned, refilled, welcomed, invited, served, refilled, gave seconds, introduced, prayed, served, refilled, sang, ate, and rested in between serving and refilling. It was a glorious dinner. When it was all over, we realized we had served more than 320 of our neighbors. We were amazed. We had just the right amount of food. There was lots of fellowship. We made many friends. The Lord was honored. It seemed like the feast to end all feasts! Cleaning up went fast as we rejoiced over the success of the evening. We all went home feeling quite blessed and satisfied.

A few days later I was still reflecting on and celebrating that great dinner. I was thinking about Jesus and His feeding of the 5,000. What a great feast that must have been! Imagine being one of those 5,000. Imagine the fellowship. Hear the stories and testimonies of how Jesus touched and healed and delivered and forgave and loved. Hear the people giving thanks and praise that Jesus came and cared. People from every walk of life, gathered together around Jesus, sharing a meal together. Struggling families. Children. Drunkards. Tax collectors. Sinners. People broken by the cruelties of life. Folks who were hungry. "They all ate and were satisfied" (Matt. 14:20; Mark 6:42; Luke 9:17). That's what the Synoptic Gospels report. They all . . . were satisfied. They all . . . were satisfied.

Then it hit me. As great as our dinner was, and as great as the feeding of the 5,000 was, our 320 and those 5,000 would be hungry again the next day. We didn't take even a bite out of world hunger, and neither did Jesus. And yet, at the end of Jesus' meal they all were satisfied. And at the end of our meal, they all were satisfied. My thoughts turned to the Kingdom. Jesus said He came to proclaim that the kingdom of God was at hand. In the Kingdom all will be satisfied. Jesus as well as the prophets before Him compared the coming of the Kingdom to a great banquet. Listen to what Isaiah has to say: "On this mountain the LORD Almighty will prepare a feast of rich food for all peoples, a banquet of aged wine—the best of meats and the finest of wines. On this mountain he will destroy the shroud that enfolds all peoples, the sheet that covers all nations; he will swallow up death forever. The Sovereign LORD will wipe away the tears from all faces; he will remove the disgrace of his people from all the earth" (25:6-8).

I don't know about you, but that sounds like a very satisfying banquet. I yearn for that. I long for it. That's the Kingdom that Jesus came to bring and proclaim.

And they all were satisfied. No, not forever. But for one meal, for one moment, they were deeply satisfied. Yes, they would have to buy bread again, but they would never be the same. In the meal that Jesus served them they had tasted the Kingdom, and they all were satisfied. Those who had eyes caught a glimpse of the coming banquet. Jesus gave them a snapshot of the future, a snapshot of the Kingdom.

The reality was hitting home that our feast to end all feasts didn't end anything, especially hunger. But for one night, for one meal, the 320 all were satisfied. No doubt that for some of those 320 there would be no turkey on Thanksgiving Day. And for many, with or without turkey, there would be strife and turmoil and sadness and tears. But they would also have a memory that the Spirit could call to mind, the memory of a moment at the Lord's table when they all were satisfied. Along with the turkey and trimmings they received a snapshot of the Kingdom. A future banquet is being planned, and the 320 already had a taste of it. We reminded them of the future. They participated in a picture of the Kingdom. That memory will call them and encourage them to persevere in seeking the Kingdom.

One hundred and twenty pounds of turkey is a lot of bird. But when it comes down to it, it doesn't go very far among hungry folks. Our church does not have great financial or material resources. The Lord supplies our needs, but so often we are overwhelmed by the needs of our community. We wish we could rid the neighborhood of hunger and homelessness and poverty. Maybe someday the Lord will give us a part in that. But for now He seems to be telling us to take the resources He does give us, even if they seem insignificant, and give the neighborhood a view of the Kingdom. Let them see a snapshot of what's coming. Give them a taste of being satisfied. I know this is the Lord's purpose for our church. We really don't have the power to do anything else. But could it be that this is the Lord's purpose for every church? To use whatever resources He provides to be a snapshot of the Kingdom? The Kingdom is coming. What more powerful thing can we do than provide a broken and hurting world a snapshot of it? For one night, for one meal, for one moment, folks of all ages, races, incomes, and backgrounds entered into the Lord's house and banqueted together at His tables. And they all were satisfied. The Kingdom is coming. I've seen a snapshot.

EXPOSURE 2:

You Are All One in Christ

𝓘F YOU WERE TO VISIT OUR CHURCH some Sunday morning, you would be greeted, at some point, by Brother Percy and Brother B. C. Brother Percy and Brother B. C. almost always sit together about two-thirds of the way toward the front on the right-hand side as you enter the sanctuary. Brother B. C. and Brother Percy love the Lord. They love to sing His praises, read His Word, and go to Him in prayer. Brother Percy and Brother B. C. truly come to church when they come to church. And they love each other, encourage each other, and lift each other up in prayer before the Lord.

But outside the Lord, Brother Percy and Brother B. C. don't have too much in common, at least as the world would see them. You would not expect to see the two of them together, or at least not together as equals. There are immense differences between them. And yet there they are on Sunday mornings, together.

This week Brother Percy is starting a new position at Carl's Junior restaurant. He was practicing his lines on everybody at church Sunday morning. Brother Percy will be helping people find a seat, making sure the tables are clean, and bringing people their orders. If they need any extra ketchup, Brother Percy will get it for them. Brother

Percy has already been working at Carl's Junior for about a year. This is a new position for him because for the first time in his life he will be a regular employee. He won't have a job coach to give him personal attention and make sure he's doing his work right. He will be on his own. He will even have to catch the city bus and go to and from work by himself. That is a big step for Brother Percy.

Brother Percy is a little challenged. Some would say he's mentally handicapped. I just say he's 37, going on 34. For the past several weeks Brother Percy has been telling me he has a birthday coming up. I asked him how old he was going to be. He said he was 37 now, and that on his birthday he would turn 34. I'm not sure exactly how old Brother Percy is, but he's somewhere in that range, and he might be getting younger.

Brother Percy loves to play basketball. He doesn't look very coordinated, but he can make baskets. His favorite team is the Bulls. He played on our church team this year. He can't wait till next season. Brother Percy loves the Bible. He won't go to Sunday School without one. Brother Percy can't read, but that doesn't stop him from volunteering. And Brother Percy loves to sing. Sometimes he knows the words and sometimes not. But he always sings. We are blessed to have Brother Percy as a member of our church.

Brother B. C. is called Dr. Cunningham most places. He has a Ph.D. in psychology from the University of Michigan. He is an ordained minister with great pastoral experience. He has had his own counseling practice as well as taught at the collegiate and graduate levels. Needless to say, Brother B. C. is well read.

This week while Brother Percy is learning to catch the bus, Brother B. C. will be speaking at a conference for pastors' wives. In fact, Brother B. C. has been speaking at conferences all summer. Brother B. C. is a powerful preacher and a highly sought after speaker. The truth is, he could be gone every Sunday with a preaching engagement if he so desired. But week after week Brother B. C. is present at our church to worship the Lord.

Currently Brother B. C. is the vice president in charge of student development at a nearby college. That is one of the highest and most important positions on campus. He is responsible for student life from housing to discipline to personal growth to career guidance. Brother B. C. oversees a staff of directors who work in all these areas. His is a job that not many folks could handle.

Much can be said about the attributes of Brother B. C. He is a highly gifted and intelligent man who has given himself to the Lord. He is a great example and constant encourager. We are blessed to have Brother B. C. as a member of our church.

Do you get the picture? In this world Brother Percy and Brother B. C. would never be together, beside each other. The closest they would get is Brother Percy cleaning up Brother B. C.'s table at Carl's Junior. Brother B. C. would always be above Brother Percy. Brother Percy would always be below Brother B. C. But at church, the two of them are together, side by side, worshiping and praising the Lord and seeking His grace. They are on level ground. They are brothers.

Watching Brothers Percy and B. C. and their love for the Lord and each other, I am reminded of Paul's words to the Galatians: "You are all sons of God through faith in Christ Jesus, for all of you who were baptized into Christ have clothed yourselves with Christ. There is neither Jew nor Greek, slave nor free, male nor female, for you are all one in Christ Jesus" (3:26-28).

Wow! Social status doesn't mean a thing in the Kingdom. In fact, there is no social status in the Kingdom, just family status. "You are all sons of God through faith in Christ Jesus." We are brothers and sisters regardless of race, education, abilities, power, prestige, and so on. That's how it is in the Kingdom. Side by side. Level ground. One in Christ.

There sit my brothers, B. C. and Percy. Their heads are bowed, and they are praying to the Lord. Percy's prayer is a little jumbled and hard to understand. B. C.'s is eloquent and clear. Both are quite moving and from the heart. Never mind that one can read and the other can't. They both are in need of God's grace. Both rely on the power of His Spirit to make it through each day. They are together, side by side, because of their mutual need and God's mutual grace. They are one in Christ. And they are giving me a snapshot of the Kingdom.

I am amazed at Kingdom life. It is so different from most of the living I see. Power, prestige, position, possessions—all those things are so important to this world. There is such a moving up and staying up emphasis in our culture, and even in the church, that we forget our deep unifying need for the mercy of God offered to us in the cross of Christ. Who is above another at the foot of the Cross? And yet how often do we try to climb, creating false divisions in the process? Oh, that we had more snapshots of Brothers Percy and B. C. They would remind the Church that she is to be different from the world. They would show the world that there is a deeper reality than personal accomplishment. There is the reality of the Kingdom, where B. C.'s and Percys are brothers, sons of God, one in Christ.

EXPOSURE 3:

When Did We See You?

WE CAN HANDLE ANYTHING for two weeks. That was our thinking as we volunteered ourselves to serve as a host site for the Interfaith Shelter Network (ISN). That meant that our church would serve as a shelter to a dozen homeless people for two weeks. We would give them a place to stay, provide them a hot meal for dinner, serve a cold breakfast, and pack a sack lunch for the day. A support congregation would help us with some of these responsibilities. We were excited to participate in the program that provides some tangible help to homeless persons.

The ISN consists of several churches and other faith communities that desire to reach out to the needs of the homeless. During the colder months (late October through March) the ISN members of each neighborhood open their facilities for a two-week period to host a dozen people. In our particular neighborhood there are two other churches that also serve as host sites. Thus, we are able to cover a total of six weeks of cold weather. After two weeks at the first site the shelter rotates to the next site for another two weeks and then on to the next for the final two weeks. Cots and bedding move from site to site.

The homeless people we serve are referred into the

program by social service agencies in each neighborhood. The agencies attempt to screen out those with problems that we are not equipped to handle, such as alcoholism, while placing in the program those who have a good chance of getting back on their feet. The host sites take care of the people at night and see to it that their food and hygiene needs are met. During the day these folks are assisted and held accountable by social workers as they seek employment and housing. It's a good program, and often people find housing. When that happens, the social service agency places new people into the program so that the 12 shelter beds stay full.

Like the Thanksgiving Eve dinner, we know that opening up our church for two weeks out of the year to host a dozen homeless people is not going to solve the problem of homelessness. Conservative estimates say that there are 5,000 homeless persons in our city, many of them women and children. It would be great to be able to build as many homes as needed for all of those people, but most of us are only a paycheck or two from being homeless ourselves. And so we help 12, knowing that we are not solving the large-scale problem, but providing hope and opportunity for a few.

The prophet Micah lived in a time when not only were people losing their homes, but their homes were actually being stolen from them. Wealthy landowners full of greed were collaborating with judges, religious leaders, and politicians who would all take bribes as they permitted the landowners to snatch land and homes away from the common class. The rich were getting richer, the poor were getting poorer, and the homeless stats were rising. Honest, hardworking folks were finding themselves left with nothing. Micah, empowered by the Lord, spoke a harsh word of judgment against these leaders and their sins. Micah knew that the Lord was just and would not allow such a society to go unpunished. And as confident as he was of

God's judgment, he was equally confident that a day was coming when "every man will sit under his own vine and under his own fig tree, and no one will make them afraid" (4:4). He saw forward to a day when everyone would have a place, a good place, and each one would be able to live without the threat of it being taken away. He was looking forward to the Kingdom, where there is no homelessness.

We look forward to that day too. As we participate in the ISN, we hope to provide a snapshot of that day. It is coming. Homelessness will have no place in the coming Kingdom. While Jesus may not have had a place to lay His head while on earth, He did tell us that He was going away to prepare a place for us, and that in His Father's house are many rooms (John 14:2). Through ISN we are able to give a few folks a very tiny glimpse of the Father's house. There is a place for them. They get a snapshot of the future.

As we are confronted by so many people and their tremendous needs, we not only look to the future coming of the Kingdom but also remember Jesus and who He identified with. In Matt. 25:31-46 we discover that Jesus identifies himself with the hungry, the thirsty, the stranger, the naked, the sick, and the imprisoned. Sounds a lot like a homeless person. Jesus calls these folks His brothers, and our reception or rejection of them is a reception or rejection of Jesus himself. Both those who receive and those who reject ask the same question, "When did we see you?"

We participate in the ISN for three primary reasons. As mentioned, it gives us a tangible way to help some homeless people get back on their feet, and it also enables us to point to that day when the Kingdom comes and no one will be homeless. The third reason is that this program helps us to see Jesus.

How many homeless persons do you know on a first-name basis? Chances are you only know them by where they hang out or by the cardboard sign they carry saying they'll work for food. After a while they all look the same, and they blend into the parking lots and sidewalks. Not only are they homeless, but also they are nameless. And we become numb to their presence, even to the point that we don't see them. And we don't see Jesus.

The ISN program facilitates us. It facilitates us getting to know some homeless people on a first-name basis. In fact, we become friends. We discover that they have names and personalities and loved ones and places where they're from and dreams and memories. They are people an awful lot like us. We are a lot like them. And as these relationships form and discoveries are made, we begin to see. And when we see, we start to care. It's no longer just fixing meals and providing a cot for the night. It's Christ.

Pearl is an older middle-aged, homeless woman who stayed in our shelter two years ago. She had a good sense of humor and was fun to joke with. She had learned to laugh at bad news. Bad news is something Pearl is quite familiar with. Life hasn't exactly been kind to her. But Pearl presses on, even though she is still on the streets today. (ISN is a good program, but it can't guarantee a home.) Often we see her downtown and stop to visit awhile. It's funny how often you see someone when you know that person's name. And it doesn't matter whether we have anything to give her or not, we just enjoy the visit.

Pearl earns some change by washing car windows. I remember one of the first times I saw her downtown after she had stayed at our church. We talked a little, and she offered to do my windows. I didn't have any change on me, so I told her, not wanting her to work for nothing. She went ahead and washed my windows and then told me something I haven't been able to forget. She told me, "I enjoy washing people's car windows, because it helps them see better." She wanted to help people see.

I imagine she wanted to do all she could to help motorists see her and her friends as they lived on the street. It was kind of a safety precaution. But whether she knows it or not, she has helped me to see. To see and not just over-look. To see that homeless persons are not just "the home-less," but that they have names. And that when I meet them, I am meeting brothers and sisters of the Lord. Indeed, I am seeing Jesus.

Wouldn't it be great if all it took to see Jesus was cleaning our windshields? It's kind of ironic, but here we are sheltering homeless people in an attempt to show that the Kingdom is coming, and here is Pearl, a homeless person, cleaning car windows because she wants people to see. Pearl helped me to see Jesus; I wonder if I helped her to glimpse the Kingdom.

I think there is a correlation there. The more clearly I see Jesus and focus on Him, the clearer picture of the Kingdom my life will present. We demonstrate the Kingdom to the extent that Jesus is at the center of our vision. If Jesus is out of focus, our Kingdom snapshot is distorted. But if we see Jesus, if our lives are truly and deeply set on Him, then our lives will be His domain. The Kingdom will be present within us. And we will be a sharply focused snapshot of His coming kingdom.

EXPOSURE 4:

The Unexpected Reversal

𝓘 WAS SHOCKED. I was angered. I was appalled. I couldn't believe my eyes. And I didn't know what to do. I just watched and listened in disbelief and animosity and shame.

I was downtown on the corner of 15th and G. I had been shopping at Smart and Final (a restaurant supply store open to the public) for a few things for the church. As I was bringing my purchases out to the van, I noticed Pearl, and we began to talk. As we visited there in the parking lot, there was a young man going around washing windshields for change. He was fairly clean-cut but obviously homeless. He looked as if he was still new to the streets—he hadn't developed a hardened look on his face yet. He was polite and a little backward as he approached people and asked to wash their windows. He had on an old, worn-out, and faded green baseball cap to shield him from the sun.

The parking spot next to my van was open. As Pearl and I talked, a man and woman in a very nice car pulled into the space. They were both well dressed and had an air of self-importance about them. The man was wearing one of those British driving caps and spoke with a sophisticat-

27

ed accent. They weren't your average Smart and Final customers, and they knew it too.

As this well-to-do couple got out of their car, the young man in the old cap humbly asked if he could wash their windows for a little change. The expensive man in the driving cap looked at him as if he were a bothersome fly and harshly told him to get lost. The tone in his voice was so fierce that we all kind of backed up. The young homeless man in the faded cap thought maybe he had been misunderstood, as if he were a mugger or a thief, instead of a window washer. So as the high-priced woman got out of the car, he reapproached the upper-class man in the sophisticated hat. He explained that he was just trying to earn some money to get something to eat. The self-exalted man in the I'm somebody cap turned and said in the coldest of voices to the lowly man in the lowly cap that he would get him a dinner in the county jail that night if he didn't get lost. With that, the high couple marched into the store, not to be bothered or soiled by such riffraff, while the rejected dirt remover wandered down the sidewalk in disbelief. He could not believe there was a man alive with such a void of compassion and kindness. And he could not believe he had ever in his whole life done anything so bad that he deserved to be treated so inhumanely.

As I left the scene, I thought of a hundred things I wish I would have said. For some reason I didn't think of a one of them while I watched the inhuman exchange. Not only was I mad about what happened, but also I was upset with myself for not being quick enough to say a word in behalf of the young man. Maybe it took a while to move from shock to anger. I don't know. The whole thing was terribly wrong.

I couldn't get what I had witnessed off my mind. I was jarred into remembering the story Jesus told about the rich man dressed in purple and a beggar named Lazarus. The story is found in Luke 16:19-31. There was a rich man who lived in great luxury. At the gate of his home laid poor Lazarus, starving and covered with sores. While the rich man enjoyed his wealth, the dogs licked the sores of Lazarus. The rich man wouldn't even give the garbage scraps from his table to Lazarus. I guess he wanted Lazarus to get lost. Scraps might have given him a reason to stick around.

But the rich man and Lazarus, as different as they were, were both men. And all men die. When the rich man died, he found himself in hell. Lazarus, on the other hand, was in heaven, being comforted by Father Abraham himself. The rich man in hell could see this and cried out to Father Abraham to send Lazarus to comfort him with some water. Father Abraham replied to the anguished rich man, "Son, remember that in your lifetime you received your good things, while Lazarus received bad things, but now he is comforted here and you are in agony" (v. 25).

What an unexpected reversal! The popular thinking was that if God blessed you in this life, it was a sure sign that you would be blessed in the next. And if you suffered in this life, it was a sign that God rejected you, and you could count on that rejection being even greater at death. But the rich man went to hell and poor Lazarus found himself with Abraham! No doubt, if the rich man would have been merciful to Lazarus, he would have received mercy. But he wasn't. He didn't have time for Lazarus. He wanted Lazarus to get lost. And when they both died, there was a great reversal that was irreversible. The lowly one was exalted, and the exalted one was brought low.

Jesus told this story to teach that the coming Kingdom would be radically different from this world. There will be a great reversal that will catch many by surprise. For some this is good news worth rejoicing about. For others it is a dire warning that needs to be heeded. But it is the truth. When the Kingdom comes, the last will be first, and the first will be last. The order of this world will pass away.

God will take mercy on those who have been beaten down, and He will crush those who have been doing the beating. The story of Lazarus and the rich man is a snapshot of what's coming.

"If you don't get lost, I'll make sure you're eating dinner in the county jail tonight!" That sure will be a costly dinner. A whole lot more than 50 cents for clean windows. Even more than the taxes it takes to employ police officers and jail keepers and judges and public defenders, such a dinner, or should I say, such an attitude, will cost the fancy-hatted rich man his very life. He is forfeiting his place in the Kingdom. He is blind to the reversal that is awaiting him. He has staked his life on the order and values of this world, not taking into consideration, or not taking seriously, the reality that the Kingdom is coming. And when the Kingdom comes, there will be a reversal.

The snapshot of the unexpected reversal is good news or bad news, depending on who you identify with. In all honesty, I find it a little scary. While I'm far from being at the top of the world financially, I am a United States citizen. That alone means I'm above most of the world. And I'm definitely better off than Lazarus and our rejected window washer. What will the reversal hold for me? Can rich men be saved?

Jesus responded to such a question by saying that all things are possible with God. He also told a young rich ruler that he needed to let go of his possessions and follow Him. As I keep in mind the story of the rich man and Lazarus, I think Jesus was telling the young rich ruler that the Kingdom's reversal needed to begin in his life *now*. If he waited until death or the Kingdom's final coming, whichever came first, he would find himself on the wrong side of the reversal. But if he embraced the reality of the coming reversal and acted upon it in this life by following Jesus and letting go of the present order with its ultimate goal of being wealthy, there would be a place for him in the

Kingdom. By the grace of God, and only by the grace of God, is it possible to embrace the reversal and follow Jesus.

Lord, forgive me for being overly concerned about a good position in this world. Forgive me for thinking I own what You have only entrusted to me. And forgive me for holding blessings tightly when I should be following You closely. Create within me a heart full of mercy and compassion. Grant me a vision of the reversal within Your kingdom, and help me to embrace it now. By Your Spirit, conform me to Your order of things. Amen.

EXPOSURE 5:

Whoever Receives You

TAYLOR, PAUL, AND SALVADOR. Almost every Friday night my wife and I have dinner with them. We've been having Friday night dinners together for nearly four years now. We've had so many dinners together that we've become friends, and I miss them when for one reason or another we don't get to have Friday dinner together.

Taylor, Paul, and Salvador aren't quite the kind of company that folks expect preachers to keep. They are alcoholics who live on the street most of the time. Our church is on 36th and National. Taylor, Paul, and Salvador often hang out in front of the liquor store on 38th and National. It's a two-block, downhill walk from the liquor store to the church. On Friday nights Taylor, Paul, and Salvador walk down to the church, and we have dinner together. We've gotten to know each other and have become friends. I think that's kind of a surprise to all of us.

I've already told you about last year's giant Thanksgiving Eve dinner. What I didn't tell you is that for the past four years we have been serving a free dinner every Friday night. The dinner is for anyone in the neighborhood who wants to come. Usually anywhere from 30 to 60 people will show up, depending on the weather and what Friday night of the month it is. No ID is required, and you don't have to sit through a sermon before you can eat. All are welcome, even those who aren't quite sober. Rarely have we had to ask someone to leave. Our purpose is multifaceted, ranging from feeding the hungry to giving mothers a break in the kitchen to being a positive place to hang out to offering fellowship to the lonely. And we don't just serve the dinner—we have dinner with those who come. Relationships are built, friendships are developed, and it's not unusual to pray with someone about hurts and hardships. We call this the table ministry. We've discovered that folks who won't come to a Sunday service will come on Friday nights and sit around the table and visit and lay their burdens down and receive encouragement. Ministry happens over the tables.

I have become acquainted with Taylor, Paul, and Salvador as a result of the table ministry. They heard about the free food, came down to the church, and enjoyed being welcomed somewhere. They have been coming back for nearly four years. They tell me one day that they'll be in church on a Sunday morning. I don't hold my breath. But I know that I'll see them on Fridays.

Sometimes they don't smell too good. Often they have the same clothes on from the week before. Usually they've been drinking. Occasionally they've had way too much. But they always respect the church, and they always receive me as a friend. They have shared their lives with me. We have laughed, and we have cried. I have carried them before the Lord in prayer. They wish they were free, but for whatever reason they remain trapped in the bottle. I look forward to seeing them. They are my friends. When they leave to go back to their home on the streets, they give me a hug and tell me thanks for caring and listening. They haven't come just to eat. They have been ministered to. They have received me into their hearts and into their lives.

In the Gospels of both Matthew and John we find accounts of Jesus telling His disciples that "he who receives you receives me, and he who receives me receives the one who sent me" (Matt. 10:40; cf. John 13:20). That is a powerful endorsement. We know that to receive Jesus is to receive the Father. But do we realize that to receive Jesus' disciple is to receive Jesus himself? When I think of evangelism and winning people to the Lord, I generally think in terms of folks inviting Jesus into their hearts and praying a "sinner's prayer." It's a really good conversion if they come to the altar during a church service and cry as they pray for God's forgiveness. Such an experience easily marks them as being born again. I'm so used to thinking of receiving Jesus in those ways that I find myself judging whether or not people are really saved by whether or not they have been saved in that way. No trip to the altar, no sinner's prayer, no salvation.

But Jesus said that whoever receives you receives Him. And He is talking to His disciples. I am one of His disciples. Is He telling me that whoever receives me is actually receiving Him? As I read it and reread it, I believe that is exactly what He is saying. A disciple is one who follows Jesus and learns of Him. Jesus is present in a disciple who is living obediently. As He says, "Remain in me, and I will remain in you" (John 15:4). So if I am living my life in sensitive obedience to Christ who is present within me, then to the degree that others receive me, they are receiving Christ. If they are open to me, they are open to Christ, who is present in me. If they are cold and closed to me, then they are cold and closed to Christ as well. If they love me and invite me into their lives and desire my fellowship, then they are loving and inviting Jesus into their lives and enjoying His fellowship. As I remain in Him, He remains in me, and whoever receives me receives Him and the One who sent Him.

That is something to think about. It means the key to evangelism isn't getting people to say the right words or have the right experience. Rather, evangelism is a matter of someone responding to Christ in their response to you as you allow Christ to control your life. It's more important to be living faithfully to Christ than to know the right words to say. This is evangelism of presence. It may lead to a conversion experience, though it may not. But salvation isn't judged by a prescribed experience but rather whether or not the disciple of Christ, and thereby Christ himself, is received.

I have a feeling that when the Kingdom comes in its fullness, we will be surprised at who's there, because there will be folks present who received us wholeheartedly but never went to the altar. I can't help but wonder if Taylor, Paul, and Salvador will be there. I hope so. I know they are looked upon as drunks and have made a lot of mistakes in life, but I like those guys. They have received me as I have been trying to abide in Christ.

Have they received me enough? I don't know. I'm glad that I don't have to be the judge of that. But I do know that they have poured out their lives to me and shared their heartaches. They have confessed their mistakes that led to drinking as well as their inability to stop drinking. They have prayed to be delivered from drinking, but deliverance hasn't come yet. They have encouraged me and made me laugh. They have loved me and my family. They received me when they could have rejected me. You know, Jesus hung out with some drunkards and sinners. They must have received Him. I sure hope I see Taylor, Paul, and Salvador in the Kingdom. Friday night dinners wouldn't be the same without them.

Not every story has a happy ending. Paul has since been shot and killed. His addictions got him into an argument with the wrong people—the police. Taylor was mugged and nearly stabbed to death. At least he's off the street now. His daughter has taken him in. Only Salvador remains, living a lonely street life of despair in the absence of his friends.

EXPOSURE 6:

Regard No One from a Worldly Point of View

$\mathcal{S}$HE WAS A FOURTH GRADE GIRL tagging along behind her sixth grade brother and all of his friends. They came to the table ministry on Friday nights to eat and play basketball. His name was Darren, her name was Erica. Occasionally their parents would come, too, but most of the time they were there on their own. Darren and Erica were your normal kids. They liked attention, and they were always looking for fun. But Darren and Erica weren't from a normal neighborhood, nor were they from a normal home. Already, as children in fourth and sixth grade, Erica and Darren were outsiders to mainstream society. It would only be a matter of time before they would show up as statistics in reports about what's wrong with urban America.

Normal is a hard word to define. It's probably not a politically correct word. Sometimes it is easier to say what's not normal than to actually identify what is normal. Normal consists of dominant values and perspectives. While it is somewhat difficult to state those values and perspectives, it is easier to spot things that don't fit with those values and perspectives. Normal is not necessarily what is right—it is a point of view. Usually those with the loudest voice and the most power within a society determine what that point of view is. It is subject to their opinion. Thus normal is a worldly point of view. Now back to Erica and Darren.

According to the world's viewpoint, Erica and Darren come from the wrong neighborhood. They are from the city. Erica and Darren do not know what it's like to live in middle suburbia, and they have no acquaintance with life in the country. They are from the city. The name of their specific neighborhood is Southeast. Have you ever heard of a suburban neighborhood named Southeast? Of course not. Such "illustrious" names are reserved for the city. Southeast doesn't have a single mainline grocery store. Only one bank has ventured to put a branch office in the community. And there's no Pizza Hut. Isn't everyone's hometown supposed to have a Pizza Hut? No, Southeast is not a good place to be from. No one will put anything good in Southeast because everyone is convinced that nothing good can come out of Southeast. Erica and Darren? The world says that they'll just be more proof of what is already known.

Erica and Darren also come from the wrong family. Their father is frequently out of work. They don't have a car. They don't have a phone. Their address has changed numerous times. They have been on the verge of homelessness, twice having to live in the worst hotel in the city. Their parents are very friendly people, but they are not well educated. And in this world, to get a good job and live high above the poverty line, it takes a good bit of education as well as a few breaks. Erica and Darren's parents haven't gotten any breaks. Thus, Erica and Darren grow up in poverty, not knowing what it's like to get an allowance or go on a family vacation. Those things are for other kids and other families. Erica and Darren are poor. The news says the poor are getting poorer. To Erica and Darren that's not news; it's a statement. It's a statement that the poor and their children have no future. There's no place for them in the workings of this world.

There is one other thing about Erica and Darren and their family that is not considered normal. They are Afro-American. They are Black. And while our country has civil rights and everyone can vote, the dominant view is that it's not normal to be Black. Laws have changed over the years, but stereotypes and images have remained. If you don't believe me, let me ask you two questions. When you observe three guys, Whites of high school age, walking together, what do you see? My guess is that you see three friends going somewhere. But when you see three Black guys of high school age walking together, what do you see? I'd bet that you see three gang members up to no good. The Black guys could be wearing the same clothes and going to the same place as the Whites, but because of their skin color you see them differently. You have a different set of expectations for them. Erica and Darren have to deal with those expectations. They grow up being looked down upon by mainstream culture because of their race. They are expected to do bad and cause trouble. The tragic thing is, if Erica and Darren accept this worldly point of view of themselves, they grow right into it. They fulfill society's negative expectations. They assume the dominant culture is right.

Allow me to spell out what society expects/suspects of Erica and Darren given their neighborhood, family, and skin color. Darren is expected to never graduate from high school. He will get involved with a gang, he will get into some trouble with the law, and he will spend some time in juvenile hall. More than likely he will father some children along the way. When he becomes an adult, the expectations don't get any better. He will be uneducated, unskilled, and unemployable. He will spend some time in jail and more time under probation. And he will be fortunate if he lives to the age of 30 without ever being hit by a bullet. From a worldly vantage point, Darren is not a good kid, and he doesn't have much to look forward to except trouble. What if Darren believes all this?

Our society's expectations of Erica are not much better. She has a little better chance of graduating from high school than Darren, but not much. The world is betting that she will get pregnant, drop out of school, and become another teenage mother. Once she has the first child, she will probably have a second child before she turns 20. Nobody will be surprised if they have different fathers. Uneducated, unemployable, and with no husband to provide, Erica and her children will go on welfare for the rest of their lives. Hopefully she will never turn to drugs as an escape from painful reality. She knows that crack cocaine will turn life into hell, but she may figure that she has nothing to lose. After all, what else is she supposed to do?

Erica is now in the ninth grade and beginning to assume that she is going to go to college. Darren is in juvenile hall for shooting someone. It seems that Darren has accepted and is fulfilling our society's expectations of him, while Erica is starting to live by a different set of expectations for herself. What brought about this drastic difference between brother and sister? Where did Erica get her new expectations? I think it's because Erica kept coming to church since those early tag-along days, while Darren quit coming, even on Friday nights, after that first summer. Christ and His church have made the difference in Erica's life. They have refused to "regard [Erica] from a worldly point of view" (2 Cor. 5:16). (Of course, we didn't regard Darren from a worldly point of view either, but I think he had already formed some worldly conclusions about himself.)

It took awhile to get Erica to start coming to church on Sundays. She never missed a Friday, but we couldn't get her there for Sunday church. We finally discovered that she would not come because she didn't think she had anything nice enough to wear. We tried telling her that she looked fine, but that didn't change her mind. So we provided some work for her to do. For her pay, my wife, Vonda, took her shopping for clothes. Since that time Erica has been one of the most faithful people in attendance in the church. If the doors are open, Erica is there.

In the church Erica is viewed and treated like nowhere else in the world. She is seen through the eyes of Christ. A Kingdom perspective prevails over the world's conclusions. Erica is loved. She is deemed important. She is challenged. And it is believed that God has far greater things in store for her than we can hope for or imagine. Erica is a special person whom God created and for whom Christ died. That is how the church sees her—not from a worldly perspective but from a Kingdom perspective. The great thing is that Erica has begun to see herself from this same perspective as well. She is a child of God. God will be with her. He will never leave her or forsake her. He made her and has redeemed her. She may have many troubles in a world that does not see her truly, but she can take heart, for Christ has overcome the world. Thus, she will not be squeezed into the world's mold for her, but she will present herself as a living sacrifice to God. And God will conform her to His image, and she will indeed be a new creation in Christ.

Do you see the role of the church in Erica's transformation? The church is a snapshot of the Kingdom. Relationships and expectations are not based upon the standards and judgments of this world. Instead, they are founded on the love and rule of Christ. The result is that every time Erica is at church, she is getting snapshots of herself that conflict with and contradict the picture of the life that the world has painted for her. She chooses which snapshots she will grow into and which vision she will ground herself in. The church, the community of believers, has brought her salvation by regarding her, not from a worldly point of view, but from the vantage point of Christ. She has found new life and new identity in a snapshot of the Kingdom.

EXPOSURE 7:

Halftime

WHEN DANIEL M. FIRST STARTED COMING to church, we would go round and round about which version of the Bible I should be using as pastor of the church. I used the *New International Version* because it was easier to understand. Daniel believed with all his heart that I should be using the King James Version. His childhood Sunday School teacher and his father both taught him that the KJV was the only real Bible and that any new Bible was the work of the devil. I kept using the NIV. Daniel kept bringing an old, old, old KJV to church. In fact, he felt so strongly about it that I was a little surprised he kept coming back to church. (I think a few of our church mothers reminded him of folks back in his home church, and that's why he kept coming.) Eventually, we sort of agreed to disagree, at least most of the time.

It wasn't long till we discovered that as much as Daniel believed in his father and his Sunday School teacher and the KJV, he did not have much of a relationship with the Lord. Daniel was serving a different god—crack cocaine.

Daniel was a plumber by trade. He was a hard worker. Sometimes he had pretty steady work with good companies. Much of the time he could only get temporary jobs or service calls. All the time he was broke. Daniel's pattern was to work hard Monday through Friday, making as much money as he could. As soon as he got his paycheck, he would cash it and start bowing down to the god of crack. Every weekend Daniel would blow his entire paycheck on crack. He was out of control. If he had money, it would all go for crack.

Yet Daniel kept coming to church, sometimes paranoid from being high, other times depressed after coming down. But he kept coming. The church family had begun to love and embrace Daniel. Daniel yearned for that love. He knew that Christ and the church were his only hope. As strong a grip as crack had on him, Daniel held on to the church.

Eventually Daniel ended up in jail. He had been in a scrape about some money with a guy and beat him up with a tire iron. The charge was "assault with a deadly weapon but not a gun." When the church learned of Daniel's trouble and court appearance date, prayer went up, and a number of us were there in court to stand by him. In brief, the result was a shorter time in jail and a bigger place in Daniel's heart for the church. He had never heard of a church showing up in court to stand by a crack addict.

Like most addicts, Daniel never wanted to admit that crack had control of his life. He would come to church and share every part of his life except his crack life. We pretty much knew what was going on, and Daniel knew we knew, but he was in such bondage that he couldn't even talk about it. He was ashamed.

Finally, after much prayer, many relation-building events, and lots of ups and downs, the day came when Daniel openly confided in us about his crack problem. We listened, talked, and prayed.

Then on a Sunday morning, at the altar, the Lord touched Daniel and set him free from crack! Daniel had been delivered! His life would be forever different! That is not to say that the desire to get high had forever left him.

But now he had the power of the Lord to see him through those times of temptation. Daniel had received a new life.

It wasn't long until several churches in our area decided to send a team to work and to witness in what used to be East Germany. As they witnessed to the people, they were to rebuild a church. The trip would take place in nine months, and they were recruiting workers. Plumbers were needed. As I heard about the project, Daniel immediately came to mind. It would be the opportunity of a lifetime and the chance to solidify the change that took place in his life. The only thing I was worried about was whether or not Daniel would follow through on a commitment made that far in advance. I didn't want to be responsible for the church spending $1,200 on a nonrefundable plane ticket to Germany and have no one go.

I presented the opportunity to Daniel. Free from crack, he didn't have anything holding him back from going—except finances and a lot of doubt that he would be selected for the team. Nevertheless, he filled out the application, and the church went to work to raise the money. To Daniel's amazement, he not only made the team but was ranked in the high priority group. To the church's amazement, the money came in for the trip. And to my amazement, Daniel followed through on the commitment.

A few of us from church took Daniel to Los Angeles International Airport to join the rest of the Work and Witness team as they awaited their flight to Germany. I never will forget what Daniel said to me on the way to the airport. We talked a little about all that the Lord had done in his life in the past couple of years. Then he said to me, "Pastor, this is halftime of my life." I knew immediately what he meant.

Halftime. A time to reflect on and learn from your mistakes, and then leave them behind. A time to develop new direction and strategy. A time to take a new course of action. A time to gain new strength and energy for the events ahead. A time to turn things around and make them right. A time to mount a comeback, so that the game is not lost. Halftime. A new game.

Daniel went to Germany and completely overhauled the plumbing of an old building to be used for a church. He also passed out several Bibles and pieces of Christian literature. He worked and he witnessed to the work of Jesus Christ in his life. It was clear to all that the Kingdom had come within Daniel.

I think about Zacchaeus. He was a tax collector who had been stealing from folks all his life. He knew he was a sinner, and so did everyone else. But he wanted to see Jesus. One day Jesus was passing through the town where Zacchaeus lived. There was a crowd around Jesus, so that Zacchaeus couldn't get to him. So Zacchaeus climbed a tree to get a glimpse of Jesus as He passed. To everyone's surprise, Jesus spotted Zacchaeus up in the tree and called him down. The whole crowd waited with anticipation. Certainly Jesus would condemn this obvious sinner who had stolen from them.

But Jesus had a different announcement to make. He was going to Zacchaeus's house with the gift of salvation. Zacchaeus gladly and joyfully received Jesus' gift and made his own announcement. He would give half of his possessions to the poor and pay back folks four times the amount he had stolen from them. It was clearly halftime. Jesus had made a change in Zacchaeus, and Zacchaeus would live differently from here on out. The Kingdom had come into Zacchaeus.

When people like Daniel and Zacchaeus experience halftime, I know the Kingdom has come. More than that, I have a snapshot of the victory that's coming.

EXPOSURE 8:

Gospeling

$\mathcal{T}$HERE IS SOMETHING SPECIAL about Christmas caroling. Gathering together to announce in song the birth of our Savior. Visiting shut-ins or nursing homes and bringing cheer to the often left out and downcast. Experiencing the unexpected lifting of our own souls by the blessings of our listeners. Having a message that's actually worthy of joyful song.

Although the Christmas season may become quite commercial and out of focus, caroling always moves us back to the center. In caroling we echo the gospel announcement of the angels to the shepherds, "A Savior has been born" (Luke 2:11). That is the special news of Christmas. It's this message that makes caroling so special.

Have you ever asked yourself why we only go caroling at Christmastime? If it's such a meaningful experience and the message is true the whole year round, why do we only do it a couple of times out of the year? Is there ever a time we don't need the good news that we have a Savior? Isn't that always worth singing about? And aren't there always folks who need to hear that song? When our church considered all these questions, we were left with an idea: Why not go Christmas caroling throughout the year?

We decided to take one Wednesday night a month and go singing. Instead of singing only Christmas carols, we would sing gospel hymns as well. Both carry the same good news that we have a Savior in Jesus. We called it "gospeling." A couple of carloads of believers meet at the church for prayer and a little warm-up of the vocal cords. Then we would go visit someone who was shut in or in need of encouragement. As we approached the door, we would start singing "Victory in Jesus" or some other familiar gospel hymn. Sometimes we would continue singing two or three more hymns outside the door for the whole neighborhood to hear. Other times we would move inside and sing the favorites of the person we were visiting. Before leaving, we would have a time of prayer in which we lifted up the person or household that we were visiting. If we had time, we "gospeled" two or three stops each time out.

One summer night we went gospeling to Brother Percy's. Percy was the only one in his household to make it out to church regularly. He also lived in a pretty rough apartment complex. We knew that as we sang to the Lord at Percy's place, a lot more folks than Percy would hear us. It was an opportunity to witness in song. In the course of our singing, a neighbor from the next apartment complained that we were too loud. Percy's apartment complex is far from a quiet place. It was apparent that this neighbor was more disturbed by what we were singing than by how loud we were singing it.

As we finished the song, the neighbor complained again. I was about ready to bring things to a close when Brother Ed started bellowing out "He Lives!" Ed and the group had taken the complaint as a challenge to their faith. Would they allow this neighbor to stop them from praising the Lord? Of course not. Everyone kept singing louder. We were taking a stand in the midst of a world against Christ. The neighbor angrily went into his apartment. Some of us looked at each other, a little worried what he might come out with. Was he going to get a gun? Ed kept singing louder and louder. All of a sudden, out came the neighbor. Our hearts stopped for a second, and then we breathed easy. He had given up the battle. He quietly took out his trash.

All the while, during this little drama, more and more neighbors heard us singing. They were glad to hear the joyful songs of salvation. We left rejoicing in the goodness of the Lord and the power of His gospel.

In the ministry of gospeling four things were taking place. First, the persons we were singing to were always surprised and encouraged by our visit. Often our visits lifted someone out of the doldrums of discouragement. Either they had felt forgotten or were feeling overwhelmed with problems. But when the church showed up, singing the powerful songs of salvation and lifting the name of Jesus, hope had arrived. Soon we were not the only ones singing. The ones we were visiting were singing and rejoicing with us.

Second, gospeling blesses not only the gospelees but also the gospelers. God does something in the person singing. Everyone who has ever gone gospeling has always come home more encouraged than when leaving. There is something about praising God and singing of His salvation with other believers that lifts the soul. But more than being encouraged, the gospeler's commitment to Christ is also deepened in the process. The gospeler puts his or her faith on the line when publicly singing of Christ's salvation. It is a step of commitment in which the believer boldly praises Jesus no matter who might be watching or listening. Gospeling ministers to the singer.

Third, we go in groups. Not only are individuals ministered to, but also the group, the Body of Christ, is built up. Relationships are grown and strengthened. The caring love of Christ is present and shared between all involved. People feel more connected with each other as well as the church. Gospeling is a unity builder.

Finally, gospeling is a witness to the world. All those in earshot hear the Good News sung that we have a Savior in Jesus. It's usually already dark outside when we go. Often there is other music in the background. But it's a hopeless music, a music without joy. Then we start singing the gospel. It's like lighting a candle in the midst of the darkness. Gospel combats the world of rap and blues. It sounds forth in the darkness, and the darkness cannot comprehend or overcome it.

The whole thing is a snapshot of the Kingdom. As Jesus made His way to Jerusalem on that first Palm Sunday, a crowd of disciples lined the road. They bowed down before Jesus and sang out praises to God. They may not have understood Jesus' kingdom yet, but they recognized that Jesus was indeed King. When Jesus was told to quiet the crowd, He responded, "I tell you, if they keep quiet, the stones will cry out" (Luke 19:40). That's how it is in the Kingdom. The King is praised and worshiped, for He has worked out our salvation.

That first Palm Sunday was not only an echo of the angels' praise of Jesus at His birth but also a preview, a snapshot, of Jesus in the fullness of His glory. In Rev. 5:11-14 we read,

> Then I looked and heard the voice of many angels, numbering thousands upon thousands, and ten thousand times ten thousand. They encircled the throne and the living creatures and the elders. In a loud voice they sang: "Worthy is the Lamb, who was slain, to receive power and wealth and wisdom and strength and honor and glory and praise!" Then I heard every creature in heaven and on earth and under the earth and on the sea, and all that is in them, singing: "To him who sits on the throne and to the Lamb be praise and honor and glory and power, for ever and ever!" The four living creatures said, "Amen," and the elders fell down and worshiped.

As we go gospeling, we stand somewhere in the middle between that first Palm Sunday and that day when we see Jesus in all His glory. We provide the world, as well as ourselves, a snapshot of that coming day. We are already singing the songs and praises of that day when His kingdom comes in fullness.

EXPOSURE 9:

One Red Tomato

ᴱARLY IN THE SPRING, right after Easter, Vonda and I began to work on our garden. Fortunately, our plot of ground in the backyard was still fairly clear of weeds and grass from the previous year. A recent rain had left the ground nice and soft. We turned over the clay soil and began to think about all the fresh tomatoes and cucumbers that we would enjoy in a few months. Of course, we would grow other things as well, such as green beans, cantaloupe, corn, and peppers. But our main crop would be cucumbers and tomatoes. Especially tomatoes. Our garden is not all that big—maybe 20 feet by 30 feet—but Vonda always sees to it that we plant more than two dozen tomato plants. We have little cherry tomatoes, giant celebrity tomatoes, early girl tomatoes, big red tomatoes, yellow pear tomatoes, and even San Diego tomatoes. If it's a tomato, Vonda is growing it in our garden.

Once the garden is planted, we must consistently take care of it. Since we don't get much rain, we have to water it nearly every day. There will be some weeding to do. As the tomato plants grow, they will have to be staked up to keep the tomatoes off the ground. Occasionally I will have to spray for bugs. Hopefully they won't be real bad this year.

After weeks of watering and watching with anticipation, summer has finally arrived, and we're beginning to reap the benefits of our work. The cucumber plants are really starting to produce. They are full of blossoms, and there are already several cucumbers ready to pick. We'll have fresh slices of cucumber on the dinner table tonight. The green beans are in need of another picking. They taste great cooked in butter. All the other plants are coming as well. The corn survived the bugs and will be ready in a few more weeks.

But still no tomatoes! And that's what we want most! Nothing compares to fresh, homegrown tomatoes in salads or on sandwiches and hamburgers. A garden's not a success without tomatoes, no matter what else might be growing. We believed that we would be getting lots of tomatoes. There were lots of yellow blossoms. But now we don't see many blossoms, and there still aren't any tomatoes.

Finally, in the midst of all the green vines and leaves we spotted a few small tomatoes! They were green and quite hard to see, but they were there. We hoped that more would be coming. Soon the garden was filled with green tomatoes! We couldn't wait to pick them!

But wait we did. There's not much you can do with green tomatoes, especially since I don't care for them fried. We kept on watering and taking care of the garden. We watched and watched. Still only green tomatoes. Would our tomatoes ripen? Would they ever turn red? Would we ever get to harvest them? Would I ever get a hamburger topped with slices of fresh tomato?

I had given up the tomato watch, but Vonda kept going out to the garden. Then one afternoon I heard a scream from the backyard. I knew immediately what it was. Vonda had found a red tomato. I ran outside. Sure enough, she had a beautiful, red, ripe tomato in her hand. There was cause to celebrate. It did not matter that all the other tomatoes were still green. We had our first red tomato. We knew a harvest was coming. We had the firstfruits to prove it. Our one red tomato was the guarantee.

The apostle Paul speaks of the Holy Spirit as being the Firstfruits of our adoption as children of God, the Guarantee of our redemption at the Resurrection. The Holy Spirit is the first red tomato. The presence of the Holy Spirit is a sure sign that the harvest is going to come. God's gift of His Spirit is His confirmation that the Kingdom is coming. It's only a matter of time. We know it's coming because we have tasted the Firstfruits.

As Firstfruits, the Holy Spirit not only affirms that the rest of the fruit (the Kingdom in its fullness) is coming but also represents the whole harvest. That first red tomato is representative of all the red tomatoes that are coming. It has the same fresh taste as the rest of the harvest. In essence, all those red tomatoes at harvesttime will be no different than that first tomato. The difference between the harvesttime and the firstfruits is that at harvesttime all the tomatoes are red. It is not a difference of kind but of measure. So it is with the Spirit and the Kingdom. Today we have the firstfruits of the Spirit in the midst of a garden full of green tomatoes. What will the Kingdom in its fullness be like? What will it taste like? It will taste like the Firstfruits, the Holy Spirit. It will be like the first red tomato. The difference will be that when the Kingdom comes in full, there will be no more green tomatoes. Everything will be transformed—not different from the Spirit we have already received but brought into conformity to that Spirit. It will not be a difference of kind but of measure.

Recently I found a red tomato in a different garden. Brother Smith had not been involved in the church for quite some time. Earlier in life he had been very active, but because of several circumstances he had sort of "retired" from the work of the church. While he was a red tomato in terms of salvation, he was a green one in terms of ministry. But then the Son must have started shining a little brighter on him. He was getting involved back in church. One Sunday morning, out of the blue, he stood and testified that the Lord had been convicting him about teaching Sunday School for our youth. I praised the Lord. We were in desperate need of Sunday School teachers. I saw a red tomato. Only the presence of the Spirit could bring a "retired" church worker back to the job. I rejoiced that I had a red tomato, not only because it in itself was so great, but also because it was an indication that the Kingdom was coming.

Another red tomato showed up unexpectedly on a Sunday night. At the close of our youth Bible study, another invitation was given to receive Christ and enter the Kingdom. It had been so long since someone had been saved in our church, I figured we would soon be closing with another prayer and another reminder that you can turn to Christ anywhere and anytime. But to my surprise and joy, Rahin, a ninth grade boy surrounded by all kinds of negative peer pressure and family difficulties, stepped forward to enter the Kingdom. He prayed the sinner's prayer and received Christ into his heart. When I saw him a week later, I knew by his smile that his conversion was real. He was a red tomato. What a blessing! I had begun to wonder if our youth would ever ripen. Now I had a red tomato to hang on to. I could see the Kingdom, even though most of the harvest was still green.

I have learned to look for red tomatoes. I need to see red tomatoes. They are snapshots that tell me that the Kingdom is coming. If I can see and taste the firstfruits, I know that the tomatoes won't be green forever. The presence of the Spirit both assures me that the Kingdom is coming and gives me a clue as to what it will be like. Thank God for those red tomatoes that keep us encouraged. Thank God for His Spirit to give us a taste of what's coming.

EXPOSURE 10:

An Acceptable Offering

$\mathcal{I}$T WAS ONE OF THOSE rare Sunday mornings when everyone made it out to church, and most folks were even on time. The song service had been lively and full of enthusiasm. After the scripture reading we offered praises and shared prayer requests. We sang another song and moved into a time of open prayer. Several people prayed out and led in Spirit-moved, spontaneous singing. When someone broke out in "Near the Cross," there could be no doubt that God was present. It was the kind of service that you pray for.

After prayer we worship the Lord with an offering, and then usually we have special music—either a soloist or a small group sings a song to minister to the congregation. Ideally, the one bringing the special music has been scheduled in advance and has had time to prepare for the service. On this particular Sunday morning, with everything going so well, Brother Ed informed me during the offering that we didn't have any special music lined up but that he was going to sing. He hadn't practiced anything or planned to sing, but he believed with the Spirit so present we ought to have a special. As music director, he took it upon himself to sing the special.

53

There are a couple of things you need to know about Brother Ed. Most importantly, Brother Ed loves the Lord. More, Brother Ed loves to praise the Lord. There isn't anything Brother Ed enjoys more than worshiping the Lord in song. Brother Ed can also play an assortment of instruments. Sometimes he brings his guitar. Other times he plays the piano. Now and then he plays an electronic omnichord. Always he sings and plays from the heart.

Brother Ed is also a security guard. He has been one for years. For most of those years he has worked the graveyard shift at outdoor sites. He has breathed a lot of cold, damp, night air. The result is that Brother Ed's voice isn't always what it used to be. Sometimes he's kind of hoarse. It's not unusual for Brother Ed to work the Saturday night graveyard shift. He gets home from work about 8:00 Sunday morning. Most folks would go to bed and not bother to get up or stay up for church. Not Brother Ed. He will be there 90 percent of the time, no matter how tired he is. Of course, this is not without effect. Sometimes Brother Ed is so tired he barely makes it through the song service—and he's leading the service! But usually the Spirit energizes him as he begins to praise the Lord.

On this particular Sunday morning that was going so well, Brother Ed had been up all night working. He was tired and hoarse, but the Spirit had touched his heart with the desire to sing and rejoice. He couldn't let this beautiful service of praising the Lord pass without a special in song. So after the offering Brother Ed stepped up to the pulpit to sing. The song he selected was one of his favorites, "My Tribute," by Andraé Crouch.

You can probably guess what happened. Ed's voice cracked from the beginning of the song clear to the end. It was very apparent that he was tired and unrehearsed. I felt bad for him, knowing that on a different day he could sing the song as well as anybody. But not this day. His voice was gone.

I was afraid that the Spirit left the service with Ed's voice. Instead of praising God, I was worried about what people would think of Ed and of our church for having such "special" music. What would I say when I got up to preach? I'm ashamed to admit it, but I was embarrassed about our musical offering.

But Ed kept singing, tired, cracking voice and all. As I watched and listened, amazed that Ed could keep on going, the Spirit began to show me something. Brother Ed was putting his whole heart into his offering of praise to God. Even though he didn't have very much on this particular morning, he was giving all that he had. Musically, it would have been counted unacceptable and worthless by most any human standard. But as an offering, it was most acceptable, for it was all he had.

The Spirit also reminded me of the story of the woman and her two pennies. As Jesus and His disciples were watching folks deposit their offerings in the Temple treasury, Jesus noticed that His disciples were impressed with the large offerings that the wealthy folks were giving. Along came a poor widow who put in two cents. Jesus quickly pointed out to His disciples that this poor widow had put in a greater offering than all the others combined. The wealthy had given out of their surplus, but the widow, out of her poverty, had put in all that she had. Her offering was the offering that pleased God.

In a day when so many people attend church with the expectation of hearing professional quality music, a day when Christians change churches because another church offers better music, a day when the pastor is embarrassed about the sound of his singers, Brother Ed is the poor widow. Out of his poverty he is putting in the greatest offering. His tired, weatherworn voice is a sweeter sound in the ears of the Lord than the productions of all the church's performing artists combined. Brother Ed is giving his all.

The Spirit didn't leave the service with Brother Ed's

voice. He came even more. I think the Spirit must have been showing the congregation the same thing. It was another snapshot of the Kingdom. In the Kingdom, the issue is not quality, but totality. It makes no difference whether we're talking music or money or anything else. In the Kingdom the question is never one of goodness, but always of allness. In many cases allness will mean goodness. But where goodness is separated from allness, when goodness becomes the criteria, we have missed the Kingdom, for there we are operating and judging only in accordance with the view of pleasing people. In the Kingdom the offering of one's all is the only pleasing and acceptable offering to God. God is watching for totality.

EXPOSURE 11:

Eating What You Plant, Dwelling in What You Build

SISTER WHITMIRE LIVES in her own place. She has lived there for about 30 years. She grows nearly everything in her small backyard—lemons, tomatoes, grapefruit, walnuts, garlic, potatoes, onions, green beans, and cucumbers, to name just a few. Anytime anyone has a cold or a cough, Sister Whitmire brings them some lemons from her tree for their throat.

Sister Tucker has her own place. She has lived there for about as long as anyone can remember. She, too, has her own fruit trees. She also has lots of plants and flowers. For Mother's Day she gave my wife beautiful flowers from her own yard.

Sister Lyne has her own place. She has lived there for about 20 years. She is a great cook. Barbecue is her specialty. Anytime there is a holiday, lots of family and friends stop by Sister Lyne's for her delicious barbecue and warm hospitality.

Brother Eric L. is a roofer. He is experienced and knows his trade well. When construction work is booming, he works long, hard hours. When construction is down, it's tough to make ends meet. Eric has put roofs on lots of other folks' places, yet he does not have his own place. He is always putting roofs over someone else's head rather than his own. He would like to have his own place, but it hasn't worked out that way.

Brother Kenny is an electrician. He is a journeyman in the field. He knows his stuff and works hard. Like Brother Eric, his work is usually feast or famine, depending on how the construction business is going. Kenny has wired lots of places for other people, but he has never wired his own place. He has no place of his own. He would like to have his own place, his own electricity to run, but it hasn't worked out that way.

Brother Marion drives a cement truck. He has poured cement for all kinds of jobs, including floors for other people's houses. But Brother Marion has never poured a floor for his own house. He doesn't have his own floor to stand on. He would like to have his own place, his own floor, but it hasn't worked out that way.

Unfortunately, Sisters Whitmire, Tucker, and Lyne are the exceptions. Brothers Eric, Kenny, and Marion are the norm. I know very few people who actually have their own place. Most folks either rent, room with someone, or live in a house that belongs to a mortgage company. Some folks are just plain homeless. Except for the very few, we're all placeless. We spend our lives building houses for other people to live in. We don't eat the crops we plant. We toil, but the fruit of our labor goes to another.

When you think about it, it's an unjust system (or a system run by unjust people) that creates a majority of people who are placeless. A relative few own most of the places. The relative few employ the majority to build those places. The injustice is that the few only pay the majority enough to borrow the places they have built with their own hands. The majority are not paid the full value of their work, for then they would be able to own the place they built. Instead, the few pocket the pay that would enable the majority of workers to dwell in the place they built and eat of the garden they planted. The few grow richer. The majority remain placeless workers.

The prophet Isaiah heard the Lord speak on the subject of the new heavens and a new earth. It was a Kingdom conversation. In Isa. 65:21-22 the Lord says of His people, "They will build houses and dwell in them; they will plant vineyards and eat their fruit. No longer will they build houses and others live in them, or plant and others eat. For as the days of a tree, so will be the days of my people; my chosen ones will long enjoy the works of their hands." In the Kingdom there will be justice. Everyone will have a place. I don't know all that the Lord means by "new heavens and a new earth" (v. 17), but justice and places are definitely a part of it.

Jesus also spoke of His people having a place. In John 14:2 Jesus says, "In my Father's house are many rooms; if it were not so, I would have told you. I am going there to prepare a place for you." Amazing. We may be placeless (and out of place) in this world, but in the Kingdom, Jesus has prepared a place for us. We will go from building houses for the enjoyment of the kings of this world to having the King prepare us a place in His house.

When Sister Whitmire picks a lemon off of a tree that belongs to her, she is a snapshot of the Kingdom. When Sister Tucker makes gifts out of her own flowers, she is a snapshot of the Kingdom. When Sister Lyne fixes barbecue in her own place, she is a snapshot of the Kingdom. For in the Kingdom there will be justice. We will eat of what we plant and dwell in what we build. In the Kingdom we will have a place.

EXPOSURE 12:

A Sprouting Seed

BROTHER ERIC G. is becoming more and more involved in the church. He started attending regularly about nine months ago. He pays his tithe faithfully, serves on our Building and Grounds Committee, and helps clean the church. One of his greatest desires is to be a good father to his two young children. The seed of the gospel is really starting to sprout in his life. He shared his testimony with our youth a few Sundays ago. God has given him a desire to help young people avoid the mistakes he made growing up.

I first met Brother Eric 7 years ago. He was about 19 years old at the time. He came to church a few times and showed up at most of our youth activities. Eric was interested in one of the girls in the church. While Eric was chasing after Shay, the Lord started chasing after him. In the following year I invested more time in Eric than with anyone else in the church. I learned that Eric was involved in gang activity and drugs. He had grown up without his father and readily admitted that most of his role models either did drugs, sold drugs, or were incarcerated. His childhood was filled with more pain than anyone should ever have to face.

In spite of his cruel childhood circumstances and the cutthroat nature of his present gang life, Eric had a tender heart. He was a people person and made friends easily. He had a concern for homeless people and enjoyed helping them. He was curious about the church and the message of the gospel. He was hungry.

Eric's gang and drug activity was increasing, but so was the hunger in his heart for a different life. We had several talks about Jesus being his only hope. Finally, at the close of a revival service, Eric came forward and invited the Lord into his life. He cried tears of repentance that turned into tears of joy. He was a new man.

It was not long until Eric faced a world of pressures and temptations. His sins were forgiven, but he was still without an honest way to make a living. He was used to making fast money, and now he had no money. His gang relations did not disappear either. Without them he had no friends. There were bonds there that were not easily broken. And while Eric wanted release from the pain of his old life, he was not yet willing to give up all the ways of that life. Within a few months it seemed that Eric was as lost as ever. He went back to the gang life.

In terms of Jesus' parable of the sower, Eric fit the part about the seed falling among the thorns. The seed fell and sprouted, but thorns grew up and choked out the seed, so that it yielded no crop. In Mark 4:18-19 Jesus explains that these are the ones who "hear the word; but the worries of this life, the deceitfulness of wealth and the desires for other things come in and choke the word, making it unfruitful." This was Eric. He wanted the peace of the gospel, but it was not his sole desire. His worldly desires choked out the gospel.

For the following five years I had all but given up on Eric. His relationship with Shay, the girl from church, had become much more involved. They had two children and were living with each other. Shay would come to church, but not Eric. I rarely saw him. Now and then I heard bits and pieces of information about him—he was still making fast money, somebody had shot at his car, he hadn't changed. I quit pursuing Eric. What was the use? He knew where I was. He knew where the church was. He knew the Way. I could not make him walk in it. It seemed I had wasted a year of ministry. Instead of winning someone, I had lost, and not only Eric but also Shay. And now there were two more children in the world whose father was a gang member and a drug dealer.

Then one November day Eric called me. He was in trouble with the law. No surprise there. He had been busted for possession of crack and was definitely going to do time. His sentencing date was in January. The only questions were how much time and where.

It's a pretty normal thing for gang members to do time at some point. It's part of the life, almost an expectation. But the Spirit had started speaking to Eric. What kind of father was he going to be to his children? Was he going to be there for them, or was he going to be absent as his own father was from him? Would his children grow up just hearing stories about him, or would they actually know him? Would he only get to see and know his children during jail visits? The Spirit really pounded away on Eric. He made it clear to Eric that he was at a crossroads in his life. Eric wanted to change.

As Eric talked, I sensed a genuineness in his voice. He wasn't looking to escape the consequences of his arrest. He wasn't calling me to ask God to somehow get him off the hook. Instead, he was prepared to do his time. He was calling me because he wanted to get right with God. He wanted God to help him change. We prayed over the phone. It seemed the Lord lifted a burden off Eric's shoulders. He felt better and said he would see me in church. I knew Eric was sincerely allowing God to begin to take charge when he really did show up in church.

During the month before his sentencing Eric and I talked and prayed several times about the changes he wanted God to make in his life. He wanted to get an honest job, even if it didn't pay as much. He wanted to leave the gang life behind, even if it meant having to change friends. He wanted to always be there for his children. He wanted to marry Shay. He wanted to be part of the church. He wanted to help other kids avoid the mistakes he made. He wanted to be right with God. He wanted the assurance that God would help him through his time of incarceration. I had no doubts about what God could do. Only time would tell what Eric would let Him do.

Eric's sentencing date arrived. With good behavior his time would amount to eight months. I wrote him and was able to visit him twice. Even though Eric was behind bars, the Spirit was working in his life. He earned his high school diploma while he was there, and he began to realize that by the grace of God he could accomplish some things in life. He began to believe that change was really possible.

The changes that Eric wanted God to bring about in his life are happening. It took him awhile to get a job, but he never went back to drug money. Once he even had to spend a weekend in jail on some bogus warrants that hadn't been cleared from the computer after he served time. Still, instead of going back to the old life, he held fast to God. Today he is a vital part of the church.

The Word is no longer being choked out by thorns in Eric's life. The soil of his life, the desires of his heart, have been turned over. I am reminded of another parable of Jesus, which is found in Mark 4:26-29. There He says, "This is what the kingdom of God is like. A man scatters seed on the ground. Night and day, whether he sleeps or gets up, the seed sprouts and grows, though he does not know how. All by itself the soil produces grain—first the stalk, then the head, then the full kernel in the head. As soon as the grain is ripe, he puts the sickle to it, because the harvest has come."

I have no idea how the seed sprouted in Eric's life; I just know that it did. God works in hidden ways. His Spirit is always working over the soil of our lives. God's work in Eric's life affirms to me that the Kingdom is coming. I can't see it. I don't understand it. It doesn't depend on me. It's not something that I can force. But the seed sprouts and grows. The Kingdom does come. Eric is a snapshot of it. I keep looking at him as I await the sprouting of more seeds. I am reminded that, in the Kingdom, the Spirit is always doing the unseen work of cultivating hearts.

EXPOSURE 13:

Blankets at New Year's

*E*very New Year's Eve a group of us from the church go on a "blanket run." We get together at the church around 8:00 in the evening, play some table games, enjoy some refreshments, and have a good time of fellowship. Everyone brings a blanket or two. Usually on the day before, I drive down to Tijuana, Mexico (not far from us in San Diego), and buy 20 extra blankets for about $80. Altogether we end up with nearly 40 blankets.

As it gets closer to midnight, we wrap up the games and begin to prepare for our trek downtown to pass out blankets to the homeless. We have a devotional and then a time of prayer. About 10:30 or 11:00 P.M. we load up in a couple of vans, dividing the blankets equally, and head for downtown. Once there, we meet in a parking lot before passing out any blankets. We form a circle, hold hands, and pray, thanking God for His grace and asking Him to watch over both us and those on the street. We then get back in the vans and drive the downtown streets, looking for those who are homeless and cold. Each van goes its own direction. We meet back in the parking lot and head for home at a little after midnight.

In San Diego, as mentioned earlier, there are an estimated 5,000 homeless people. Many experts believe the number is significantly higher. As we drive around the streets of downtown, it is not very difficult for us to find someone who is homeless. Many of those who are homeless have been on the streets so long that they have become professionals at surviving street life. They have acquired sleeping bags, blankets, carts for their belongings, and a network of friends who watch out for them. As we drive around, we look especially for those homeless persons who appear to be the most vulnerable. We search for those who have no blankets, who have only cardboard or less for cover. We look for the ones who are alone, who have no network of protection. We look for the needy among the needy.

When we find someone sleeping on the sidewalk without a blanket, we slowly approach them. Only two or three get out of the van. We do not want to startle or scare them. We don't want them to feel as if a gang is approaching. We ask if they could use a blanket. They almost always say yes with much gratitude and appreciation. There have been a few times when people have turned down a blanket and pointed us in the direction of someone in greater need. Those have been humbling moments. If they are open to it, we visit with them a little before going to the next person. Occasionally we get to pray with them. They almost always know we are a church group without our saying a word. At times the people are so out of it that they don't respond to us. We gently put a blanket over them before we leave.

We recognize that we do not accomplish very much with a blanket run. Forty blankets do not go very far toward solving the problem of homelessness. I don't know that receiving a blanket from us has ever changed anyone's life. To my knowledge, we haven't won anyone to the Lord. So why do we do it?

We need to do it for our own salvation. But for the grace of God, many of us would be homeless. It teaches us to be thankful for what we have. More than that, we learn to recognize Jesus. Jesus speaks of the homeless as His brothers. When we give a blanket to a person who has nothing, we are giving a blanket to Jesus. Though we are passing out blankets to homeless persons, we are meeting, serving, and worshiping Jesus. The activity serves to correct our perspectives and deepen our understandings of both Jesus and folks who are homeless. It tenderizes our hearts to both Jesus and people in need. That's a good way for us to start the New Year.

But that's not all. In Deut. 24:12-13 Moses is giving the Word as to how the people of the Lord should live in the land when it comes to making loans and taking pledges. The Word is, "If the man is poor, do not go to sleep with his pledge in your possession. Return his cloak to him by sunset so that he may sleep in it. Then he will thank you, and it will be regarded as a righteous act in the sight of the LORD your God." In verse 17 it says, "Do not . . . take the cloak of the widow as a pledge." A person's cloak (or blanket if you will) is that one's last line of defense against the cold of night. To deprive one of his or her cloak is to leave that one vulnerable and discount his or her value. It is a dehumanizing affront to personal dignity. Moses is saying that if you make a man a loan, and he is so poor that all he can give you for a pledge is his blanket, you have to return it to him before sunset even if he has not yet paid you back the loan. No matter how poor or in debt he is, he has a right to a blanket at night. He has the right to protection from the cold. And the widow is guaranteed her cloak. It is not even to be taken as a pledge during the day.

When we give a blanket to one who is poor and without a cloak, we are restoring a measure of that one's dignity and worth. Though the person may still be overwhelmingly poor, he or she is at least counted as human. In the Kingdom everyone is of value. The weak are to be cared for and protected, not trampled upon. God champions the cause of the vulnerable. He sees to it that they have a blanket of protection. In the Kingdom, no one has to fear the cold.

In the Gospel of John, Jesus uses the Greek word *paraklētos* in speaking of the Holy Spirit. "Counselor," "Advocate," "Helper," and "Comforter" are all used to translate this word. *Paraklētos* is a noun that comes from the verb *parakaleō,* which literally means "to call alongside of, to help and encourage." The Holy Spirit comes alongside us (and within us) and counsels us, helps us, encourages us, comforts us, and is our Advocate in time of attack. The Holy Spirit is the believer's defense against the cold of the world.

Sometimes we call heavy, quiltlike blankets "comforters." They cover us and shield us from the cold. They make a cold night more comfortable, almost giving a sense of security. When we give persons a blanket, we are coming alongside them to encourage them, help them, and comfort them. Our putting a comforter over them is somewhat symbolic of the Comforter that Jesus seeks to give them. He wants to blanket both them and us with His Spirit.

Our blanket runs are snapshots of the Kingdom, for in the Kingdom no one will be without dignity, and no one will be without the Comforter. We don't try to explain all this with every blanket that we pass out, but somehow people know. The Spirit is subtly at work, reminding both giver and receiver of the future. And that's why each year we distribute 40 blankets among 5,000 homeless people.

EXPOSURE 14:

Father-Rooted Forgiveness

THE OLD TESTAMENT is full of interesting stories about God's people and His dealings with them. Often these stories contain snapshots of the Kingdom. We don't always see them because either we think we already know the story or we're so caught up in trying to figure out the story (and how and if it could really happen) that we miss the picture.

One such story is the story of Joseph, found in the Book of Genesis, chapters 37—50. At the beginning of the story we are introduced to Joseph and his 11 brothers. They are the sons of Jacob. Joseph is number 11 of Jacob's 12 sons. He is also Jacob's favorite. Out of his favoritism Jacob has given Joseph a special "coat of many colours" (KJV), which serves as a constant reminder that Joseph is the favorite.

As might be expected, Joseph and his brothers do not dwell together in unity. The brothers are jealous of Joseph. Moreover, in his dreams Joseph sees all of his brothers bowing down to him. He is exalted over them. Joseph does not remain quiet about his dreams. He matter-of-factly informs his brothers that he will be master over them. This creates utter rage in his brothers' hearts against him.

One day the brothers found themselves alone in the

field with Joseph. He was beyond the protective hand of Jacob. The brothers believed that this was their opportunity to get rid of Joseph. Some of the brothers wanted to kill him. Reuben, the oldest, intervened. He did not want to be responsible for the shedding of his brother's blood. But not wanting to miss out on their opportunity, the brothers threw Joseph down into a pit until they figured out what to do. When a band of merchants traveling to Egypt came near, they decided to sell Joseph to them as a slave for 20 pieces of silver. The brothers covered their sin by taking Joseph's special coat and making it look as if he had been attacked and killed by a ferocious animal. They dipped the coat in goat's blood and presented it to their father. Jacob was convinced that his favorite son had been killed by a wild beast. He mourned for many days.

As the story unfolds, we find that the Lord is with Joseph, even as a brash young man sold into slavery. Having been humbled, the Lord exalts him to a high position in Egypt, then humbles him again by allowing him to be cast into prison under false charges, and then exalts him to an even higher position. Joseph ends up being in charge of all the food in Egypt. This is quite significant, for there is a famine in the land. It means that Joseph is the most powerful person in Egypt.

Joseph's brothers could not escape the famine. They had no idea what became of Joseph, but they knew there was food available in Egypt. Jacob sent them down to Egypt to ask for grain. It came about that Joseph discovered that his brothers had come seeking relief from the famine. He met with them and, after much drama, finally revealed himself to them. His brothers' lives were in his hands, just as he had dreamed. He moved his brothers and his father to Egypt and saw to it that they were well cared for. The famine did not touch them.

By now Jacob was quite old. It was not long before he died. Upon his death a wave of fear came over the brothers.

Would Joseph have them executed for the sin they committed against him? Had he really forgiven them, or was he just waiting until their father passed to get revenge? He certainly had the power to order their deaths. What could they do to spare their lives?

The brothers decided to fabricate some final instructions from their deceased father. In Gen. 50:16-17 we read, "So they send word to Joseph, saying, 'Your father left these instructions before he died: "This is what you are to say to Joseph: I ask you to forgive your brothers the sins and the wrongs they committed in treating you so badly." Now please forgive the sins of the servants of the God of your father.' When their message came to him, Joseph wept."

As the story concludes, we find that Joseph did indeed forgive his brothers. He recognized that what his brothers had meant for evil, God meant for good.

Think for a moment about the brothers' plea for forgiveness. At first it seems that it is just a deceptive ploy to save their lives. We tend to look down on them for lying, for putting words into their father's mouth. Ignore that and focus on the dynamics of their plea. They are not asking Joseph to forgive them on their own merit. They know that they do not deserve to be forgiven. What could they ever hope to do or say to make up for that day when they sold their brother into slavery? Neither are they asking Joseph to forgive them on the basis of his own heart. They do not believe he has love enough for them, in and of himself, to show them mercy. Rather, they ask Joseph to forgive them on the basis of their father. They hoped that because Joseph loved his father, he would be loyal to his father's will—even if it meant forgiving the brothers who sold him. Though there was a chasm of wrong between them, there was the prayer that an appeal to their common father would bring reconciliation and restore their brotherhood. They knew that forgiveness was rooted in their father.

Forgiveness rooted in the Father. That's how it is in

the Kingdom. The Kingdom is full of forgiven and forgiving people. All the forgiveness that takes place is rooted in the Father. No one is righteous enough to deserve forgiveness. No one is loving enough to naturally forgive. But forgiveness takes place because of the Father. He moves one child to seek forgiveness and the other child to offer forgiveness. Reconciliation is possible because they are of the same Father.

Earnie and Johnathon had a deep grievance between them. Once brothers in the Lord, their relationship had been destroyed. All unity had been lost. The Father was not pleased with what He saw. Soon the Spirit went to work prompting Earnie to reach out to Johnathon in search of forgiveness. That was a major step. There was no reason in the world why Earnie should have hoped that Johnathon would forgive him. Why humble himself and ask for it? But the Father was not content to let this relationship lie in ruins. The Father brought Earnie to the point of seeking reconciliation with his brother. Had it not been for the Father, Earnie would have never turned back toward Johnathon.

Johnathon was too hurt and too angry to offer Earnie forgiveness. Even though Earnie sought reconciliation, Johnathon would not accept him. He just did not have it in himself to even shake Earnie's hand. This was hard for the Father to take. The Spirit began working on Johnathon. Not only did Johnathon have no peace with Earnie, but also now he had no peace with the Father. He was reminded of how much the Father had forgiven him. The day finally came when, out of a desire to have peace with the Father, Johnathon began to seek peace with Earnie. He opened his heart and received Earnie back as his brother. The Father smiled. He was making progress in the work of forgiveness between two of His children.

The Spirit keeps working. The Father knows it will take awhile for the reconciliation to be complete. Trust and warmth are not rebuilt overnight. But the construction is well underway, for the cornerstone of forgiveness is now in place.

That's how it is in the Kingdom. We all hurt and have been hurt. We are both the cause and the victim of alienating deeds. But in the Kingdom, hurt and alienation do not have the final say. There is forgiveness—Father-rooted forgiveness. The Father supplies each child with the desire and grace necessary for reconciliation. Moments of forgiveness, be they Old Testament stories or present-day dramas, are snapshots of the Kingdom.

EXPOSURE 15:

Jesus Is Our Peace

O N A STORM-THREATENING JANUARY Sunday morning, in the midst of the NFL playoffs, two small churches did something that went largely unnoticed in a city caught up in the drive to the Super Bowl. Lakeside Church of the Nazarene hosted San Diego Southeast Church of the Nazarene for a combined worship service. Yet for those who had eyes to see, they were viewing a snapshot of the Kingdom.

The Lakeside Church is located in the somewhat rural community of Lakeside, which is roughly 30 miles to the east of San Diego. While suburbia has enveloped Lakeside with freeways and housing developments, the community has maintained its rural character and feel. It still hosts a rodeo. It is couched in the foothills. The land around the small lake is largely undeveloped. Downtown is historic. The population is not very diverse, being predominantly Anglo, and the church reflects this. San Diegans tend to stereotype the people of Lakeside as rednecks who drive pickup trucks equipped with gun racks.

San Diego Southeast Church of the Nazarene is located in an inner-city neighborhood to the southeast of downtown San Diego. There are few Anglos in the community. The population of the church is predominantly African-

American. The reputation of the neighborhood includes violence, gangs, and drugs. It's not exactly considered a desirable place to live. Tourists don't come to San Diego to visit our part of town.

What do southeast San Diego and Lakeside have to do with each other? Nothing. The communities for the most part are mutually exclusive. Thirty miles apart, the members of either community are out of place in the other community. There are barriers erected along the line of culture, income, race, transportation, education, politics, and taste in music. The stereotypes associated with each community don't exactly bring down the walls. But don't get me wrong. Though they look down on each other, it is not as if the two communities are at war with each other. Rather, they have nothing to do with each other, and there is no desire to have anything to do with each other. They are two separate communities, two peoples.

What do Lakeside Church of the Nazarene and Southeast Church of the Nazarene have to do with each other? Good question. Aside from the mutual denominational affiliation, given that the one is in Lakeside and the other in southeast San Diego, it would appear that they have nothing to do with each other. There are too many cultural barriers between the communities that have become comfortable and acceptable, even to the good church folk in both communities. Both churches keep to themselves and go about the business of being a church.

One day at a denominational gathering, Rev. Steve Morely, the Lakeside pastor, starting talking to me about the commonalities of our respective churches. That was new thinking to me. All I could imagine was 30 miles of walls. Steve pointed out that both churches are relatively small and roughly in the same financial situation. Both churches are composed of members from their communities, and both seek to proclaim the gospel to their communities. In a sense, we are two churches on the same journey but in different communities. We spoke of becoming sister churches that might encourage each other along the way.

It's one thing to speak of being sister churches; it's another thing to develop sisterhood. Our congregations did not know each other. There had been no avenues for interaction. We decided to hold a combined Sunday morning worship service at the Lakeside Church as a first step toward sisterhood. Hopefully it would go well, and there would be future combined services where we could encourage each other in the work of the Lord in our communities.

As the day of the combined service approached, we began to realize that it was not only a day to encourage each other but also a day to bear witness to and actually demonstrate a dimension of the gospel message that is often left unsaid and undone. It was an opportunity to proclaim the truth that Jesus is our Peace in a way that neither congregation could do by itself.

A church's membership often reflects the kind of people that compose its neighborhood. Sometimes, however, a neighborhood changes, population groups shift, and a church of one kind of people finds itself meeting in a neighborhood of another kind of people. In either case, the church's membership tends to be composed of one particular kind of people. This tends to subtly imply that the church (including its message and Savior) is for only one kind of people. As we confess with John 3:16 that "whoever believes in him shall not perish but have eternal life," we visibly communicate that "whoever" means "whoever is like us." We do a poor job of bearing witness to the truth that the gospel is for all peoples when our local churches do not move beyond the barriers that divide peoples.

Paul, in his letter to the Ephesians, writes that Jesus is our Peace. We usually think of this in terms of Jesus being our Peace with God. If it were not for God reconciling us to himself through Jesus, we would be alienated from God and forever in rebellion. Jesus' death on the Cross was God offering peace to us. It opened the door for us to live in right relation to God.

As true as all this is, it is not what Paul had in mind when he wrote that Jesus is our Peace. The context reveals that Paul was dealing with the relationship between Jews and Gentiles. Jesus is the Peace between Jews and Gentiles. He broke down the barrier that divided the two kinds of people. This barrier had fundamentally to do with access to God. Jews, God's chosen people, descendants of Abraham, and recipients of the Law through Moses, had access to God. Gentiles (everyone who was not a Jew) did not enjoy such privileged access to God. They had not been given the Law. The Law functioned as much as a community identity marker as it did a way of life. It became a barrier of hostility between the two kinds of people. Jews felt superior because they had the Law. Gentiles scoffed at the Jews and their peculiar regulations. There was no peace between the two peoples.

When Jews and Gentiles formed the Early Church, they brought their attitudes with them. Jews still felt superior because they had the Law (which to them meant superior access to God). Gentiles still scoffed. Paul writes to move the church to peace. He doesn't mean a cease-fire kind of peace, but a peace of reconciled and healthy relationships. His chief argument is that in Jesus the barrier between the two peoples no longer exists. In Jesus, Jews and Gentiles have equal access to God. They are now one. There is no ground for conceit or ridicule. The barrier of the Law has been brought down. It can no longer function to divide people before God. Paul informs the church that Jesus' death on the Cross made peace a possibility and demands it be a reality. Jews may be Jews, and Gentiles may be Gentiles; but in the Church, because of Jesus, the two peoples are one. There is horizontal reconciliation and peace in Jesus.

Jesus is the peace between kinds of people. He has

brought equal access to God to every group, nation, race, family, and so on, on the face of the earth. In the presence of God there is no room for scoffing or conceit. Every people can come to the Father through the Son.

But how often do we bear witness to this truth? When we worship in congregations of only one kind of people, we present a view of the Kingdom tainted by the barriers that exist in society. It has been said that Sundays are the most segregated day in America, and that the Evangelical church is the most segregated place in America. It's terrible that such a statement can be made about the church. But who can deny it? And yet our gospel proclaims that Jesus is our Peace, and that we are one people before God. We don't do a very good job of giving people a view of the breadth of the gospel. The snapshots we provide have a lot of brothers and sisters cropped out of the picture.

On that seemingly ordinary January Sunday when two small churches worshiped the Lord together, something extraordinary happened. It wasn't the music. It wasn't the sermon. It wasn't the offering. It wasn't even the prayer time. It was simply who was there, who was in the picture. The walls were brought down for a day. Blacks and Whites from two mutually exclusive neighborhoods gave expression to the truth that Jesus is our Peace. Together we did what we could not (at this point) have done by ourselves. We were a snapshot of the Kingdom in which no one was cropped out by the barriers of society.

Oh, that we had more such snapshots. The world needs to see them.

EXPOSURE 16:

Holy Love

I MET SISTER LYNE about eight years ago. She and her husband, Frank, would make it out to church usually a couple of Sundays a month. That was quite an accomplishment because Brother Frank had multiple sclerosis and was confined to a wheelchair. It was not long until Brother Frank's condition worsened, and he couldn't get out of the house at all. As his pastor, I tried to visit Frank once a week. He had a remarkable spirit. Bedridden, he still had a sense of humor, a love for the Lord (and baseball), and the ability to spread joy. Though Frank and Lyne were not able to make it to church services, they continued to pray for the church daily.

I visited Frank and Lyne almost weekly for four years. During that time MS took over more and more of Brother Frank's body. He was in and out of the hospital often. In 1991 he went home to be with the Lord. It was a day full of both grief and joy.

Frank and Lyne have three adult children. The oldest daughter, Denise, also suffers from MS. She, too, is confined to a bed or wheelchair. She has little strength and has virtually lost the ability to speak. Sister Lyne and her dear friend, Sister Cathy, take care of Denise. It is a never-ending work of compassion that often leaves them weary.

I am amazed at Sister Lyne's love and devotion to her family, especially the way she cared for Frank. Why did she pour herself out for Frank? Why didn't she put him in an institution that would take care of him? These were the years of life that she should have been able to enjoy. Frank was in the navy, and as a military wife Lyne had to virtually raise the three children by herself. It had not been easy. She had no family in the area to help her. But she did it and did it well. Having given herself unreservedly to her family for years, she deserved some time to live for herself a little. Instead, she found herself tied down to taking care of Frank and suffering the grief of seeing his health go from bad to worse. Why did she hang in there with him? Why didn't she find some other option so that she would be free to enjoy life? And now she is doing the same thing with Denise?

I suppose that she did (and still does) it all because of love. But it is an unusual kind of love. Unusual because, from the world's perspective, Frank (and Denise) went from being lovable to "unlovable," and yet Lyne's love and devotion increased instead of decreased. I say "unlovable" because there was nothing tangible about Frank that made it worthwhile for Lyne to give him such demanding care. He could not respond with the same active care that she gave him. He couldn't return what he was receiving. This put Lyne in a very lopsided relationship. She constantly had to deny herself and put Frank first. Frank's needs always had to be met. In return he could only offer gratitude and appreciation. Lyne had to live her life around Frank. It was not the life that either of them had envisioned or dreamed of on their wedding day.

So why did Sister Lyne love Brother Frank so much? I suppose it has to do not so much with Brother Frank but with Sister Lyne. Sister Lyne loved Brother Frank and displayed such devotion to him because of who she is. She was simply living true to her own (God-given and transformed) character. Sister Lyne was just being Sister Lyne. That's why Brother Frank was so loved and well cared for.

When I consider Sister Lyne's love for Frank, I get a snapshot of the love of God, the love that brings the Kingdom. God loves us not because of who we are, but because of who He is. His love is grounded in himself, not in our lovableness. He loves us because He is holy. Holy love is rooted in the Giver, not the receiver. That is what makes it holy. That is what makes it love.

The prophet Ezekiel knew about this kind of devotion. In Ezek. 36:22, 24-27, 29, 32 the prophet delivers this shocking message of salvation.

> Therefore say to the house of Israel, "This is what the Sovereign LORD says: It is not for your sake, O house of Israel, that I am going to do these things, but for the sake of my holy name, which you have profaned among the nations where you have gone. . . . I will gather you from all the countries and bring you back into your own land. I will sprinkle clean water on you, and you will be clean; I will cleanse you from all your impurities and from all your idols. I will give you a new heart and put a new spirit in you; I will remove from you your heart of stone and give you a heart of flesh. And I will put my Spirit in you and move you to follow my decrees. . . . I will save you from all your uncleanness. . . . I want you to know that I am not doing this for your sake, declares the Sovereign LORD."

Ezekiel delivered this message to the Israelites in a time of despair and hopelessness. God had sent His chosen people into exile because of their sinfulness. He raised up the Babylonians to deliver His punishment upon them. The Babylonians conquered the Israelites, destroyed Jerusalem, and burned the Temple. They carried off the Israelites and forced them to live in captivity in Babylon. It was a bitter time.

Ezekiel's message was one of good news for the exiles. It contained the promise that God was going to magnificently save them. He was going to restore them to their homeland, take away their disgrace as a people, and bless them with prosperity. Even more, He was going to cleanse them, give them a new heart, and put His Spirit within them that they might live righteously. They would indeed be God's people. What an awesome promise!

But notice the motivation behind this incredible salvation. It has nothing to do with Israel and everything to do with God. He opens and closes His promise with the stern words that it is "not for your sake" that He is going to save them. God is saving them for the sake of His holy name. God is going to save them, to continue on in devotion to them, because He is true to himself. Israel has nothing to offer Him. Their devotion has never matched His devotion. It has been a lopsided relationship from day one. And yet God is committed to delivering and restoring Israel. Why? Because God is God; He is holy. He loves and saves out of His own character. That is the hope, the only hope, of Israel, for she is unlovable. That is Israel's gospel.

That is also our gospel. The Kingdom comes because of God, not because of us. God does not offer us salvation in Christ because of what we have to offer Him but because He is His holy self. His devotion to us is rooted in His character, not ours. It is a lopsided relationship. All we can offer is gratitude and appreciation. God so loved us and gave His Son for us, because God is God.

In a world in which love rises and ebbs on the desirableness of the beloved, it is easy to lose sight of the most powerful love of all, holy love. Holy love is rooted in the Giver, not the beloved. It is the love that drives the Kingdom. It originates with God. It transforms His people, but not in such a way that they suddenly have something to offer Him in exchange for His love. They begin to love because of the change God has brought about in their character. Having His Spirit, they love because of who they are in Christ. Love is no longer about giving and receiving. It is about who you are.

Unknowingly, Sister Lyne in her devotion to Brother Frank has given us a snapshot of the Kingdom. In the Kingdom, love is holy. The King loves because He is holy. Having received His holy love, we are to love in like manner. They will know we are His by our love.

Sister Lyne wrote a poem to express the prayer of her life. I believe the Lord has heard her prayer and is answering it.

Delight

Delight I want to do in You, Lord.
Help me to be only for You.

I want to delight in You, Lord.
When the path seems rough,
Help me to be tough.

I want to delight in You, Lord.
When Satan comes my way,
Help me never to stray.

I want to delight in You, Lord.
In the midst of my troubles,
Make me a blessing to others.

I want to delight in You, Lord.
In prayer, in thanksgiving, in praise,
Will You direct my every phrase?

Help me, dear Lord, to delight and look up,
For my determination is to never give up.

EXPOSURE 17:

One Who Pours

S HE IS ONE OF THE STRONGEST WOMEN I know; she is one of the weakest women I know. She is old and frail and feeble; she is lively and powerful and bold. I have seen her taken advantage of, yet hurt does not overcome her. She battles arthritis, cancer, surgery, and chemotherapy. Her body gives little indication of winning, yet she lives victoriously. She has her days of weariness and discouragement, yet she is constantly encouraging and lifting others. Her income is low, and she gives much of it away, yet there is nothing lacking in her. She gives definition to generosity while living in poverty. Her name is Sister Tucker. She is very human and very saintly.

Sister Tucker is best known as a pray-er. When she is on her knees, she touches heaven. She gets through to God. People have the confidence that when Sister Tucker prays, God listens. I wouldn't want to say that she gives orders to God, but she certainly lets Him know what she thinks needs done.

There is nothing that Sister Tucker does not pray about. She holds nothing back from God. She tells Him when she is discouraged. She tells Him when things are not going right and when people are not doing right. She prays, expecting God to work, to make a difference in the matter. She does not prescribe solutions that limit God as she pours her heart out to Him. Rather, she remembers that God is God, thus leaving open the door of hope for Him to work beyond her imagination and in ways not immediately discernible. She has an honest, trusting relationship with God. She knows that He is her Strength and her Salvation.

Sister Tucker not only brings needs to God but also receives direction from Him. She does not live her own life. She takes chances on helping people that common sense says to have nothing to do with. Why? Because God directs her to. She speaks to people she doesn't know, sometimes about the gospel, sometimes about the things she perceives about them or sees them doing. She has actually confronted gang members about their drinking and hanging out on the streets, letting them know that she loves them and that God loves them. Why? Because God directed her. She counsels people, carries the burdens of others, and does not live to or for herself while being at an age and in a state of health that would suggest retreating and retiring. She remains in San Diego, doing the missionary work that God has called her to do, instead of returning to her family roots in Florida. Why? Because God is directing her life.

Sister Tucker has more "adopted" children and grandchildren than anyone I have ever met. People in need come to her (or she is directed to them). They find a caring soul who will cry with them and admonish them in the ways of the Lord. She gives hope to young people while sprinkling in sermons on doing right. She shoulders the burdens of numerous young and middle-aged adults. And she especially befriends the aging and dying, those battling terminal illnesses. It seems Sister Tucker has a gift of mothering—from brokenness to healing, from sin to salvation, from despair to a brighter day.

Sister Tucker pours out herself to God and people in

need. In that pouring is a snapshot of the Kingdom, for Kingdom life is a pouring life. Think of Jesus. He poured His heart out to God; He poured His blood out for sinners. Jesus spent 40 days in the desert following His baptism in preparation for His ministry, praying. During the course of His ministry He retreated from the crowds to spend time in prayer. At the close of His earthly ministry He prayed for himself and His disciples. In the garden He wrestled with His Father's will for the Cross. On the Cross He cried out, "My God, my God, why have you forsaken me?" (Matt. 27:46). From beginning to end, Jesus emptied out His heart to His Father. There was nothing He did not bring before God. He carried the needs of the people before God, as well as His own needs, struggles, and questions. Kingdom life is a life of pouring ourselves out to God.

Jesus, out of His relationship with His Father, poured himself out in ministry. He met people at their point of need. The woman at the well comes to mind. Jesus was tired and hungry from the day's journey. Along comes a Samaritan woman whom Jesus perceives to be in great need. Instead of ignoring her, He ministers to her, quenching her thirst with His Spirit. He poured himself out. He became the Well from which she drew.

Of course, the ultimate outpouring of Jesus was the Cross. There Jesus gave His body and blood that every one of us, no matter how unworthy, might receive life. There is no greater expression of love than that a man lay down his life for another. Charles Wesley, picking up on the thought of the apostle Paul, penned these lines about Jesus: "Emptied himself of all but love, / And bled for Adam's helpless race" ("And Can It Be?"). Jesus poured himself out completely. He gave His life to us. Kingdom life is a life of giving ourselves to others.

It needs to be noted that while Jesus poured out himself to God and humanity, He was never confused about whose He was. He gave himself to people, but He belonged to His Father. His Father gave Him instruction and direction, not mortals. He did not permit men to make Him an earthly King. Men and women did not determine His schedule. He lived in obedience to His Father. His giving of himself to people was always in the context of obedience to His Father. Jesus' pouring himself out to His Father always determined the nature and course of His pouring himself out to humanity. Kingdom life is a pouring out life. As we pour ourselves out to our Father, He directs us in pouring ourselves out to others.

Sister Tucker helps me to see this "pouring out" quality of Kingdom life. She provides me a snapshot of the way Kingdom people live. Her authentic witness and demonstration of Kingdom life is of the greatest value. This is so, not only because her whole way of life can be characterized as a pouring out, but also because she is so human. She's old. She has arthritis. She is weak from cancer, surgery, and chemotherapy. Sometimes she wonders why the Lord is keeping her in San Diego instead of letting her go home to Florida. As much as she would like, she can't fix everything and everybody including herself. And she knows it. She is human.

And yet, in the midst of her humanness and her weakness, she keeps on pouring. She empties her heart to God; she shares her heart with neighbors. No matter how great the need or burden, Sister Tucker will come alongside and help carry it to God, arthritis and all. The apostle Paul writes in 2 Cor. 4:7-11 that

> we have this treasure in jars of clay to show that this all-surpassing power is from God and not from us. We are hard pressed on every side, but not crushed; perplexed, but not in despair; persecuted, but not abandoned; struck down, but not destroyed. We always carry around in our body the death of Jesus, so that the life of Jesus may also be revealed in our body. For we who are alive are always being given over to death

for Jesus' sake, so that his life may be revealed in our mortal body.

So often we think we have to be strong in order to be pourers. We think that we have to become something other than human, or at least something other than our human selves, before we can embark upon the poured-out life. And so we spend our time and energy trying to look and become strong, instead of just pouring. Paul and Sister Tucker would agree that people thirsting for life don't need us to be a silver pitcher—they just need us to pour. They would also agree that we have nothing to pour, except as we pour out ourselves to God and receive from Him. The pitcher remains human. It is the drink that is divine. The presence of the Kingdom is not indicated by pitchers but by pourers.

Sister Tucker is a constant reminder that Kingdom life is a pouring out life in the midst of our humanness. It is pouring out ourselves to God and neighbor in our own weakness.

There is another woman made famous for her pouring. Her name was Mary. She poured a pint of expensive perfume over the feet of Jesus and wiped His feet with her hair. John recalls that when Mary did this, the whole house was filled with the fragrance of the perfume (12:3). Her single act of devotion changed the air of the whole house, the air that everyone was breathing. People couldn't help but notice the invading presence of her relationship with Jesus. As Sister Tucker pours out herself to God and neighbor, not only does she give us a snapshot of the Kingdom, but also the whole neighborhood is filled with the fragrance of the Kingdom. The scent of her devotion is in the air. People can't help but notice that there's a Kingdom coming.

EXPOSURE 18:

The Light Shines in the Darkness

ER EYES ARE BRIGHT with the love of the Lord. She is a strong and steady Christian with a genuine compassion for others. She always greets people with a smile whether or not she knows them. Her desire is to win people to Christ. Her strategy is to become friends, pray for the person, and trust the Spirit to prompt the person to ask her about her own life, why she is different from most people. She tells of the Lord and what He means to her, never pushing religion onto another person, but always giving an invitation to know and trust Jesus.

I remember when she started coming to our church. Her family had moved to San Diego from Colorado. The Lord led them to attend and participate in His ministry at Southeast. She always sat on the third row on the right side. She was very alive and in tune with the Spirit throughout the service. Worship in prayer and song flowed from her heart. As I preached, I sensed that she was following the sermon closely. She had a deep hunger for the Word, and it was as if she couldn't get enough of the gospel. Anytime I needed an "Amen" of affirmation, all I had to do was look in her eyes. Her eyes lit up in response to the Truth.

Her ministry at our church included befriending anyone who came through the doors, praying for folks throughout the week, and encouraging the pastor. Her presence was a vital part of the services. Now we are having to make do without her.

I miss her. She has grown a little older, has moved away from home, and now has her own ministry. In this new ministry the Lord continues to shine in her life, perhaps brighter now than ever. She has given herself to ministering to those confined to live in the Del Capri Convalescent Home.

Hers is a ministry that most of us would not want. There is little glory in it, few people notice her, and the rewards are obscure. She spends her days befriending those who have been forgotten by their own families and loved ones. Many of these folks have lost the capacity to care for themselves. They find themselves and their needs at the mercy of overworked staff. Even worse off are those who have lost their mental capacities to communicate and remember. They live out the remainder of their lives in an isolated world. Often the hallways echo with the groanings of one who is deranged and in anguish. This is the world in which she lives and ministers. I know of few darker places.

And yet "the light shines in the darkness, and the darkness has not overcome it" (John 1:5, margin). She continues to greet her "parishioners" with a smile and eyes that communicate the love of Jesus. She is not drowned by the ocean of needs that surround her. She is not in despair over her inability to fix these aged and worn-out people. Rather, she keeps on trusting in Jesus as she prays for people and shares the gospel story. She is a Christlike reminder of the love of God among a people that have been largely forgotten.

I have purposely withheld this woman's name from you, partially because hers is a nameless ministry, but more so because I wanted you to be free to form your own image of her. I suspect that as I described her and her ministry, you imagined a young woman in the prime of her life, very bright and full of joyous energy, eager to go wherever Christ sends her. You most likely imagined a young woman full of enthusiasm that would light up any roomful of folks, young or old. Well, the name of this woman is Sister Green, she is pushing 90 years old, and she lives in this convalescent home because her family can no longer provide her the care that she requires. Though her eyes are bright, her body is shriveled. Though her faith is strong, her legs are weak. She can barely walk. Most of the time she is in a wheelchair. Though her lips speak of Jesus, her mouth has few teeth, and a stroke has left her jaw slightly out of place. She has had two close calls with death. Once I began mentally preparing her funeral message. There is no doubt that she is approaching the end of life. Her body is all but worn-out. And yet the Light shines in the darkness, and the darkness does not overcome it.

Sister Green has unknowingly reminded me that in the Kingdom the Light that shines is Jesus, not we ourselves. What shines the most about Sister Green is Jesus in her. She herself is past the days of shining. The aging process has been hard on her. And yet her eyes are bright with Jesus. She truly sees the convalescent home as her field of service during these days of her life. She would rather be home, but that is not a realistic possibility. So she goes about her days befriending others who, like her, live in wheelchairs and hospital beds. She prays for them and looks for opportunities to tell them about Jesus. She is a missionary in a dark land. She has no light to offer except Jesus.

One of the songs we learn to sing as youngsters in Sunday School is "This little light of mine, I'm gonna let it shine." (Our daughters started learning this song before reaching the age of two.) While we know and teach that Jesus is the Light, and that we are light only to the extent that Jesus is in us, I think we get confused about what it means to let our light shine. It doesn't help that we live in a day of stars and superstars, of camera lights and flash-bulbs. There is a tendency to equate shining with being at the peak. Professional athletes shine for only a few years while they are at the peak of physical conditioning and mental preparation. Once their abilities begin to deterio-rate, they no longer shine. Someone else who is peaking assumes the spotlight and becomes the center of attention. A new star begins his or her short season of shining. The same thing happens in the entertainment industry, the business world, the school campus, the social circle, and so on. The one who shines is the one who is peaking, the one who is rising above the field in the designated area of com-petition. Such shining has little to do with Jesus and every-thing to do with the development of human strength, knowledge, and beauty—usually for self-serving purposes.

While the development of God-given human abilities has its place (in the loving of God with heart, mind, soul, and strength, and not in the exalting of oneself), peaking is not to be equated with shining in the Kingdom. Peaking puts the spotlight on human achievement. In Kingdom light, Jesus shines, regardless of where you are in relation to peaking. A problem arises when a peaking mentality in-vades our understanding of letting our Kingdom light shine. This mentality actually puts our light under a bowl so that others cannot see it. The bowl comes in several shapes, forms, and sizes. There is the bowl of striving, into which all the resources of life are poured in an effort to achieve success, to reach a peak. There is the bowl of main-tenance, into which all one's energy is poured in the at-tempt to hold on to a peak, to keep from slipping down the other side. Then there is the bowl of despair, filled with the realization that the peak is out of reach, perhaps in the past, perhaps unattainable all along. What these bowls have in common is a focus on personal shining rather than Jesus shining. The effect is to conceal the light of Jesus and magnify ourselves.

I think we tend to think that if we shine, Jesus will shine, and that if we're not shining, Jesus can't shine. So we pour ourselves into shining, doing everything to mask or overcome our frailties that might keep us from the peak. And in the process we hide the Light. Sister Green, long past peaking, full of undeniable frailties, has come to grips with the truth that she has no more days of personal shining. And yet the Light shines in her.

Sister Green is another shapshot of the Kingdom. She helps me see the light of the Kingdom. It is the light of Jesus, not our personal peaking and shining. It is a Light that shines when we don't and perhaps can't. It shines in the darkness, and the darkness cannot overcome it.

EXPOSURE 19:

Who? Where?

*R*EV. MERLE GRAY. You've heard of him, haven't you? He has been a minister of the gospel for 50 years. You say you haven't heard of him? Well, surely you've heard of the church he is pastoring. He's the senior pastor at Cocopah Church of the Nazarene in Somerton, Arizona. Somerton? That's about 10 miles south of Yuma, about 10 miles north of the Mexican border, about halfway between San Diego and Phoenix. Still haven't heard of him or his church? Neither had I until last week. I was part of a team that helped work at his church and witness in the community.

Pastor Gray and his wife, Ruth, have been pastoring the Cocopah Church of the Nazarene for four years. The church ministers to the Cocopah Native American tribe, whose reservations are in the Somerton area. The tribe has more than 500 members. The church runs about 50 in attendance on Sunday mornings. It is not an easy place to grow a church.

Pastor and Mrs. Gray have virtually given their lives in ministry to Native Americans. Out of 50 years of ministry, 40 have been to Native Americans in one capacity or another. Along with pastoring, Rev. Gray has served at an Indian Bible college in Albuquerque, New Mexico. When the Grays first accepted the call to minister to the Native Americans, it involved moving from Pennsylvania to Oklahoma. The move left Ruth extremely homesick and depressed. They returned, to discover that she had tuberculosis. She nearly died. But the Lord saw her through to recovery and then healed her homesick heart. She asked her husband when they were heading back to the reservation. She was ready to go. Brother Gray told me that since that day, Ruth has never complained of homesickness.

Pastor and Mrs. Gray live in a church-owned parsonage about 100 yards from the church's sanctuary. The church covers the cost of their utilities and pays him a salary of $400 a month. Not bad for someone with 50 years of experience. Ruth works 20 to 30 hours a week at the Yuma K Mart to help make ends meet.

In the week I was with the Grays, I never heard them complain about their lot in the ministry. They still possessed a love for the people and a love for the church. Pastor Gray still made the rounds picking people up for church on Sunday mornings and spending time in prayer for them during the week. Their love flowed across the generations to the children and youth of the church. Their humble and faithful service was an inspiration to me. It also forced me to evaluate my own motives and ambitions as a servant of the Lord. After 50 years of service and a calling that nearly cost me my wife, would I be content to pastor the Cocopah Church of the Nazarene if that's where the Lord called me?

To be honest, I don't know. I hope I would be. But I must admit that after 50 years of ministry I'd like to have an assignment that's a little more . . . well . . . prestigious. Don't get me wrong. I want to serve the Lord wherever He calls me, and I'm not looking to climb the ecclesiastical corporate ladder. But after 50 years I hope to have at least a minimum of tangible success—something I can point to with a little "sanctified" pride. I would like to be at a place where I would receive lots of applause and accolades from my brothers and sisters in ministry for a job well done. Hopefully those under my ministry would be extremely appreciative and grateful to have a minister of such experience. And I'd also like to be able to live comfortably, not having to worry about making ends meet. Would I be willing to take the Cocopah church after 50 years of ministry? Not on my own. The Lord would have to help me.

But there are the Grays. Fifty years of service to the Lord, their names virtually unheard of, and in a final assignment that very few care about. There is no crowd cheering them on as they approach the finish line. They have run the race, and the stands have been largely empty. There is no prestige. There is little glory. They have spent their lives ministering in obscurity, and they will complete their ministry in obscurity. And they keep on loving the people and serving the Lord.

In that obscurity is a snapshot of the Kingdom. Applause, prestige, and recognition are not essential ingredients to ministry in the Kingdom. The accolades of humankind, even the church, are not necessary for the minister of the Kingdom. The Kingdom minister works in response to the Lord. The ambition of the Kingdom minister is to please God. Recognition from colleagues and parishioners, while enjoyable, is not the aim. The ultimate and controlling desire is to hear the words, "Well done, good and faithful servant!" (Matt. 25:21, 23).

Such noble ambition is rooted in the One who calls. The Lord knows His servants. He knows who He has called, and He remembers where He has placed them. There is no assignment that is obscured from His vision. He sees the ministry that is done in secret. No good deed escapes His notice. He will not fail to reward.

I need this liberating truth to sink deep within my heart and permeate my whole being. There is no need to pursue recognition and affirmation from any quarters, including the church. It is God himself who recognizes and affirms. He never forgets His servants, regardless of how out of the way their assignments might be. His memory is good, His vision unobstructed. He is faithful to His servants. He does not fail His ministers. He promises to be with us always, even unto the end of the age (Matt. 28:20).

The Grays remind me there is a Kingdom, and it is coming. They are out of step with the ambitions of this world. The only explanation is that they are keeping step with the coming King.

God, please grant that I might keep step with You—and the Grays.

EXPOSURE 20:

These Feet Stink

$\mathcal{I}$T HAD BEEN A LONG THREE DAYS. Everybody's feet stunk. It started late Thursday night, getting packed for a mission trip. I, along with Brother Mack and five teens from our church (Ty, Mickey, Rahin, Myisha, and Erica), would be going to Chilchinbeto, Arizona, to do some work for a church there. Chilchinbeto is located on the Navajo reservation and is about an hour southwest of Four Corners. Our work included putting in a sidewalk, repairing the church's roof and fencing around the church property, tiling some floors, putting in parking berms, and remodeling the church's entranceway. We didn't know exactly what all our work would entail, nor what tools were on hand, so I was busy packing every tool I owned. Friday afternoon Mack and I picked up the kids as they got home from school. They were giving up their spring break to go on this weeklong trip. Our 1978 15-passenger Dodge van was loaded as we hit the highway. Only prayer would get us from San Diego to Chilchinbeto.

The mission trip we were going on was part of Project YES (Youth Equipped to Serve), a spring break Work and Witness ministry sponsored by Point Loma Nazarene College (PLNC). Project YES teams up high school kids from all over California, Arizona, and New Mexico with adult leaders and PLNC students and sends them on mission trips to either Native American churches or churches in Baja California, Mexico. Usually a team consists of about a dozen high school kids, a college student or two, and three adults serving as site leader, construction foreman, and cook.

We were heading to Barstow, California, Friday night to meet the rest of our team. We would spend the night on a gym floor and hit the road again early in the morning. We wouldn't arrive in Chilchinbeto until late Saturday night. It would be a full day of travel, fast food, gas, stretching, and bathroom stops.

We arrived so late Saturday night that we didn't have much idea of where we were or what the church was like. All we knew was that it was cold and windy, with sand blowing everywhere. After a good night's rest on the church's floor, we awoke to fresh air, bright sunshine, and a beautiful day. We were in the high desert. We got cleaned up (as best as we could) and ready for a full day of church. The services were in Navajo. I preached both morning and evening with the help of a translator. The afternoon was a time for catching up on some sleep, figuring out the work for the week, and exploring our temporary home.

I felt good about our team. We were quite diverse, and yet we were coming together. Our team consisted of three kids from the Fresno area, two from near Santa Barbara, two students from Nazarene Indian Bible College, a kid from New Mexico, a PLNC student, a kid from northern California, a woman also from northern California who served as cook, and the seven of us from San Diego. Genderwise, we had six teenage girls, six teenage guys, two women, and four men. As for ethnicity, we were three Native Americans, six African-Americans, and nine Whites. As you can imagine, we came from several different walks of life. And yet here we were, in the middle of nowhere, getting to know each other and care for each other, preparing to work together for the Lord and His church as a team.

There were several memorable moments on the mission trip, but for me, the snapshot moment came on that Sunday night after all the church folk had gone home and it was just us. The team gathered together in a circle to discuss plans for Monday and then close the day with some devotional time. I went into the kitchen and came back with a large pot of warm water and a dish towel. The kids were trying to figure out what was going to happen. I went to Mickey, untied his shoe, took it off, pulled off his sweat sock, and started washing his foot. After washing his foot and drying it off, I told him that Jesus set us an example and told us to go and do likewise. He then took the towel and the water and proceeded to wash someone else's foot, telling that one the same thing. The towel and water were passed around until everyone's foot had been washed.

At first the kids mildly protested having to wash someone else's foot or having to let someone wash theirs. Either scenario was somewhat embarrassing. We had been going almost nonstop since we left Friday. No one had had a chance to really get cleaned up from the long journey. The church did have showers for us, for which we were very grateful, but not all the kids had had a turn to use them yet. Even those who did shower left with dirty feet. We weren't staying at the Holiday Inn. Once past the initial protests there was joking and laughter about all the stinking feet. Eventually there was thoughtful meditation about what we were doing. Jesus showed us His love by humbling himself, putting on a servant's towel, and performing the lowliest of household tasks. Then He told us to go and do likewise, to follow His example. He taught that people would recognize us as His disciples by our love for one another.

We had come to Chilchinbeto as the Lord's disciples. We were there to improve the facilities of the Chilchinbeto church and hopefully be a blessing to the people. The only way we could do it was if we followed Jesus' example. We needed to be humble enough to serve each other, humble enough to work together, humble enough to care for one another. Only by loving each other in such a Jesus-like way would we distinguish ourselves from just another construction crew. We were there because of Christ. The only way we could bear witness to Christ was to love—to become foot washers.

There are images from that foot washing service that remain alive in my mind. White hands washing black feet. Black hands washing red feet. Red hands washing black feet. Black hands washing white feet. White hands washing red feet. Red hands washing white feet. The towel and water being passed back and forth between hands of different shades, textures, and sizes. Some hands were well cared for and soft. Some hands were rough and hardened by work and weather. Some hands showed signs of past injuries that never quite healed right. Some hands were used to the feel of money. Some hands weren't used to touching another person. And all the different feet from so many walks of life, ranging from city streets to sidewalks to country roads to desert terrain. So many differences and so much in common. Every foot needed to be washed. Every hand was capable of washing. That's one reason hands were created—to wash another's feet.

Love was present. Jesus was alive. Somehow His love brought us together to love and serve one another. Had it not been for Jesus, none of us would have been there, and none of us would have loved. Economic, racial, and a host of cultural barriers would have kept us apart. But there we were, washing each other's feet. The gospel makes people do strange things.

As we washed each other's feet, I saw a snapshot of the Kingdom. In the Kingdom, the example of Jesus is followed. Love is manifested in practical, mundane, and even embarrassing deeds of service. Social position, status, and barriers are tossed aside. All feet need to be washed. All hands are called to wash. The simple outpouring of love awakens people to a new reality, a new world. It's the Kingdom. And when I see foot washing, I know it's coming.

EXPOSURE 21:

Baptism

$\mathscr{B}$APTISM AND THE LORD'S SUPPER are the two clearest expressions of the Kingdom the Church possesses. Each time one of these sacraments is received, both believers as well as the world are given a snapshot of the Kingdom. In the sacraments we receive the Kingdom, and it is only in receiving the Kingdom that we can be a manifestation of the Kingdom. The sacraments declare that the Kingdom is coming.

Baptism is the sacrament of initiation into the Kingdom. The baptism of an individual (whether by dunking, sprinkling, or pouring, it makes no difference) testifies before the Church and the world that this person believes in Jesus and that God has received this person into the Kingdom. Baptism bears witness to the baptized's faith and even more to God's grace and faithfulness in providing salvation in establishing His kingdom.

This latter point is especially important. The Church baptizes believers as a sign of their entrance into the community of the saved. It is a rite of initiation, a symbol of entering a new life under a new realm. If it were not for God's prior work of bringing His kingdom in Jesus, baptism would be meaningless. There would be nothing to be baptized into, no new community, no new life, no new realm.

Usually we think of baptism as testifying to the baptized person's coming to faith in Christ. This it does, but in doing so, it testifies to much more. It reminds us of what God has done in Christ to bring His kingdom and make salvation a reality. There is a Kingdom to be entered. Baptism puts this truth before our eyes. It is the snapshot of the moment of initiation. Here are two of my favorite baptism photos:

It was a great day for going to the beach. The sun was out, the sky was blue, there was not much wind, and the temperature was in the mid to upper 70s. We loaded up the grill, packed a couple of ice chests full of hot dogs, fixings, and drinks, and headed for Mission Bay. We were ready for a summer afternoon of sun and fun at the beach.

But this was no ordinary trip to the beach. We were going as a church, and we were going to conduct church business. There would be lots of swimming and playing, eating and lounging, but there would also be some very serious and joyous business to attend to. We would be holding a baptismal service for both our new and our unbaptized believers. We figured there was no better place to do it than in public before God, nature, church, and San Diego. So following the Sunday morning service, we hurried out to Mission Bay.

Since we were conducting Kingdom business, Brother Cunningham and I decided to remain clothed in our church garb. The water was a tad bit chilly as we waded out to waist depth. The general public wondered what we were up to, dressed in our Sunday best and standing in the middle of Mission Bay. Our baptizands were on the shore, waiting to be called into the water. The church was gathered around them. One by one, Brother Cunningham and I called each person. Each one slowly waded out to meet us in the water. We individually asked all of them if they had confessed their sins and invited Jesus into their heart, if they knew Him as their personal Savior. We prayed with them for God to do His work in their lives. Then with

Brother Cunningham on one side and me on the other, we rocked them back into the water and baptized them in the name of the Father and the Son and the Holy Spirit.

All the baptizands went under the water with a little apprehension. I'm not sure whether they didn't trust us to bring them up, or they weren't sure what all they were getting themselves into. Following Christ almost always involves more than we initially realize. But when they emerged from the water, their faces told a different story. They were radiant with joy and bright with new life. It was a Kingdom moment. Their baptism testified to all who could see that God's kingdom is coming and that by His grace they had been received into it. They no longer belonged to the realm of the world that is passing away. Their place is in the Kingdom.

Not all of our baptisms are in the Pacific Ocean. Neither are they all submersions. One Sunday morning we baptized little Carlos. He was about nine months old. I held him in my arms before God, the church, his mother, and his mother's family. After praying for him and his mother, I sprinkled water over his head, baptizing him in the name of the Father and the Son and the Holy Spirit.

That was the first time I baptized an infant. Some folks don't think infants should be baptized—only dedicated. Their reasoning is that baptism is one's testimony of personally deciding to follow Jesus. A baby is simply too young to make such a decision. No one should be baptized until he or she is old enough and mature enough to actually choose to follow Jesus, so the thinking goes. Only after making such a mature decision should one be baptized. It's OK, on the other hand, for babies and children to be dedicated to the Lord. That is a testimony to the decision of their parents. Dedication leaves children free to make their own decision about Christ when they come of age. Dedication does not involve the child's will. The integrity of baptism is preserved.

But baptism is not so much a testimony of a willful decision to follow Jesus as it is a witness to the saving grace of God and belonging to His people. Wesleyan scholar Rob Staples, in his book titled *Outward Sign and Inward Grace*,* has helped me to understand this truth. Baptism testifies to God receiving, by His grace, the baptized person into His kingdom, His family. Children and babies, unable to make moral decisions, are yet received by God. The mentally handicapped, unable to make cognitive faith decisions, are received by God. Baptism is the appropriate witness to this receiving. God's saving grace extends to these people. It does not hinge on their capabilities to make rational and moral decisions. God receives them into His family by grace. Baptism is the sign of their reception and belonging.

For little Carlos, the implications of his baptism are especially important. Carlos is growing up without a father. His parents were not married when he was conceived, and his dad did not want the responsibility of raising a son and caring for a wife and family. Little Carlos is blessed with a mother who loves him and several relatives who help care for him, but his family is far from complete. He will grow up under the cloud of a father who rejected him and his mother. He was born with a huge hole in his life.

The gospel for Carlos is that even as his dad was rejecting him and running from him, God was declaring through the sacrament of baptism that there is already a place prepared for him in His family. Little Carlos's baptism communicated the truth in tangible and visible ways that he belongs to the family of God. He can call his Maker Father. As he grows up wrestling with the actions of his dad, his mother and the church can remind him of the loving action of his Father. God took him into His family, even as his dad had nothing to do with him. He is a recipient of God's grace. There is a place for him in the Kingdom.

---

*(Kansas City: Beacon Hill Press of Kansas City, 1991).

Of course, as Carlos grows, he will have to make decisions about following Jesus. Infant baptism is not an automatic pass into heaven. It does not free one of accountability to the Lord. But instead of having to choose to become part of the family of God, Carlos will be faced with the choice of remaining part of the family of God. It is a subtle difference, but a difference for sure. It means he grows up under the testimony of God and all who were present at his baptism that he has a Father and family who are proud of him and who desire him. He grows up belonging, instead of having to join. His baptism is his snapshot of proof. Hopefully, when he is of age, he will choose to continue to belong. In the meantime, I can't imagine a better way to grow.

EXPOSURE 22:

The Lord's Supper

O<small>N THE FIRST</small> S<small>UNDAY</small> of every month we celebrate the Lord's Supper. It is the church's ongoing testimony to the Kingdom. It is a time of community and personal definition. We remember Jesus. We receive Jesus. We open ourselves to the transforming grace of God that we might become more like Jesus.

The sacrament of Communion has several dimensions. Remembering, thanking, receiving, committing, witnessing, and hoping all intersect in this one event. Each dimension is significant to the formation of Kingdom people.

Remembering the sacrificial and atoning death of Jesus is usually the dominant emphasis of the Communion service. We remember that on the night Jesus was betrayed, He was gathered at the table with His disciples. "While they were eating, Jesus took bread, gave thanks and broke it, and gave it to his disciples, saying, 'Take and eat; this is my body.' Then he took the cup, gave thanks and offered it to them, saying, 'Drink from it, all of you. This is my blood of the covenant, which is poured out for many for the forgiveness of sins'" (Matt. 26:26-28). As we reenact this meal, we reflect on the sacrifice Jesus made as He went to the Cross on our behalf. He died for our sins that we might be forgiven. Our iniquities were laid upon Him, and it is by His wounds that we are healed. He literally laid down His life for us that we might live.

Such remembering reminds us that our citizenship in the Kingdom did not come at a cheap price. Kingdom membership is not to be treated lightly. It also informs us that our Kingdom citizenship is not the result of our own merit. We are an unworthy people. We have sinned. We fall short of the glory of God. Christ, the sinless One, became sin for us, that we might be reconciled to God. The words of Peter come to mind: "Once you were not a people, but now you are the people of God; once you had not received mercy, but now you have received mercy" (1 Pet. 2:10). In the Supper we remember the cross of Jesus.

As we consider the death of Jesus and our own unworthiness, our hearts are filled with thanksgiving to the Father. "For God so loved the world that he gave his one and only Son" (John 3:16). It was God's initiative to send Jesus to die for us. He desired our reconciliation. He chose to make us His people. As Paul says, "God demonstrates his own love for us in this: While we were still sinners, Christ died for us" (Rom. 5:8). Thus the Lord's Supper is commonly referred to as the Eucharist, which comes from the Greek word *eucharisteō*, which means "to give thanks." As we take the bread and the cup, we give thanks to God for the gift of salvation.

In the process of remembering and giving thanks, we come to an ever deepening knowledge of God. We discover afresh that God takes sin seriously. He does not ignore it. He does not pretend that we are righteous or that our rebelliousness will simply go away on its own. God deals with our sinfulness. He paid the full price of forgiveness. He sent Jesus to the Cross, revealing the magnitude of the Cross within His own heart as He seeks our reconciliation. God accomplishes our salvation—not because sin is a small thing, but because He is a great God.

As we hold the bread and the cup in our hands, we also discover afresh the amazing truth of how God saves. He comes down. He descends. He enters in. He saves from within. He does not remain an outsider. He becomes one of us. "The Word became flesh and made his dwelling among us" (John 1:14). "That which was from the beginning, which we have heard, which we have seen with our eyes, which we have looked at and our hands have touched— this we proclaim concerning the Word of life" (1 John 1:1). God may be "up there," but He comes "down here" to save us. He meets us where we are. He's not afraid to get dirty. He meets us in the wounded flesh and bleeding of life. That's where we live, and that's where He comes. "'They will call him Immanuel'—which means, 'God with us'" (Matt. 1:23). The bread and the cup, common and earthly as they are, reveal to us the incarnational, saving ways of the Divine. The Kingdom is not to be left on high. God desires to bring it, on earth, as it is in heaven.

Communion is received. The elements are not just held and thought about. We eat them. We take them in. The elements represent Jesus. He is not just to be studied and pondered, He is to be received. Communion is for the Lord's disciples. As we take the bread and the cup, we are opening ourselves to receive more of Jesus into our lives. We are inviting Jesus to invade our lives with His presence and to establish His rule within us. We are committing to follow Him, to obey Him, to imitate Him. We confess that the only way we can fulfill this commitment is if He lives within us. We need Him. In Communion we seek and receive His transforming presence into our lives.

Communion is received together. The disciples did not eat with Jesus individually. They were together with Jesus, gathered around a common table. They shared the Passover meal together. As we celebrate the Lord's Supper together, we bear witness that regardless of income, education, race, or anything else, we are one people in Christ. We serve the one Lord. We serve Him together. He is our vertical and our horizontal Peace. He draws us together, exposing as well as meeting our common need for grace. Were it not for Him, we would not be a people, we would not be eating together. Our eating together testifies to the world of His presence. Only He could draw such an unlikely band of folks together around a common table.

While we're at the table, we discover we need not only Jesus but also each other. The table fellowship encourages us and transforms us in our walk with Jesus. We minister to and receive ministry from each other. The result is that Christ is formed within us as individuals as well as a community. By our love for one another the world will know we are Jesus' disciples. Love isn't manifested when a believer is alone. It becomes visible only in the context of being together. At the table, love is shared with the bread and the cup. The meal is a witness.

As we celebrate the Lord's Supper at our church, we try to pay attention to each of these themes. Sometimes they are more pronounced than others, but always the dynamics are at work. There is one other dynamic that we have especially begun to recognize. It is the future dynamic of hope. The Supper not only reminds us of the death of Jesus but also points us forward to the coming of Jesus. It is a preview, a reminder of the future banquet that is coming.

It was a common metaphor in Jesus' day that the kingdom of God would be a feast. In Luke 14:15 an unnamed character proclaims, "Blessed is the man who will eat at the feast in the kingdom of God." Jesus picks up on the metaphor and tells the parable of the Great Banquet in verses 16-24. Here Jesus supports the banquet theme but calls the listeners to rethink their understanding of who will be in attendance. At the Last Supper, Jesus seems to have this messianic Banquet in mind when He tells His disciples, "I will not drink of this fruit of the vine from now on until that day when I drink it anew with you in my

Father's kingdom" (Matt. 26:29). Thus, Jesus' last supper with His disciples was not just pointing *to* the Cross but also *through* the Cross to the future messianic Banquet to be held when the Kingdom comes in its fullness. The Church also looks forward to this Banquet, and with each celebration of the Lord's Supper the Church proclaims that the Banquet is coming. There is cause for hope. The Kingdom is coming. The Supper is a taste of it.

The recognition of this future dynamic has changed the way we celebrate Communion at our church. We actually celebrate. We sing songs like "When We All Get to Heaven" and "When the Roll Is Called Up Yonder." We are reminded that in the midst of our unworthiness and the struggle to work out our salvation, we have a future hope. No matter how unfriendly the world, no matter how distasteful the plate before us, no matter how tough the battle, we have a banquet to attend. There is a place set for us. We have cause to sing.

When we are discouraged, when we are wondering if the Kingdom is ever going to come, when hope is running low, we can accept Christ's invitation to come to the table. There we will remember and give thanks, receive and commit, love and bear witness. And we will go forth with hope, having seen a snapshot of the Kingdom.

EXPOSURE 23:

The Group Shot

$\mathcal{I}$T'S TIME TO GATHER EVERYONE in for a group shot. So far we have focused primarily on individuals who in some way reveal the presence of the Kingdom. There are countless more individual photos that could have been presented, but a roll of film only has so many exposures. As we come to the end, a group shot of the believers at the church I pastor is in order. You have been reading, for the most part, about isolated members or events at Southeast. But the Church does not exist in isolation, and neither does the Kingdom come in isolation. The Kingdom comes, the Church exists, in the middle of life; and life is full of problems, joys, connections, and a vast range of relationships. Individual shots never tell the whole story. Group shots, for that matter, usually leave someone out. But the group shot at least makes the assertion that there is a group. Reality is bigger than one. There are always people who live and work behind the scenes that need to be included in the picture.

Group shots are always telling. Not everyone makes it into the front row. Not everyone wants to be in the front row. There are always people who are partially hidden. Only an arm or a shoulder or a leg makes it onto the film.

There are those who are caught off guard and embarrassed about how they look. And there's always someone who's missing but is nonetheless part of the group. The picture makes the statement that this is who we are—hair out of place, blinks, rabbit ears, and all. We exist together. We are a part of each other.

The Southeast group shot is no different than any other group shot; not everyone is captured by the camera. I apologize for not being able to squeeze everyone into the picture, because all are vital to the church, belong, and are recognized as one of us.

As we scan the Southeast group shot, we notice Sister Cathy, who leads a Thursday morning Bible study for the patients of a convalescent home. She also gives daily care to one of our shut-ins. There is Sister Whitmire and the Glaze family who helped start the church in 1961. They contribute immeasurably to the life and ministry of the church. Hiding in the back row is Brother Mack and his family. Sister Gloria helps care for Sister Tucker. The two of them get together for prayer every Tuesday. Brother Mack drives the church van week in and week out, demonstrating more patience than I've ever seen. Next to him is Miguel, a young man called to the ministry who is especially gifted with the ability to minister to our neighborhood youth. To the left is Sister Marion. She touches lives everywhere she goes. She always brings a ray of hope to the hurting. Beside her is Alexandra and her baby Darius. Alexandra grew up in the church, went off to college, and now has come back to finish up her schooling here in town. It's rewarding to see her remain in the church and participate in the church's ministry. On the other side is Barry, Jody, and little Barry. Jody serves as treasurer, and Barry organizes our monthly men's prayer breakfast. The prayer breakfast is one of the ministries I enjoy most.

Toward the front are a number of youth. Over the years, Southeast has always reached out to young people.

Two bear special mention, for they were young people who reached out to other young people. Myisha and Michelle, unrelated and of different generations, never came to church alone. They always brought with them siblings, cousins, friends, and neighbors. A person is never too young (or old) to be used by the Lord.

To the right are the four people who keep me most encouraged—my wife, Vonda, and our children, Rebecca, Rachel, and John Mark. Vonda is my companion in ministry. I do little without her being involved in some capacity. She is my sounding board, my chief editor, my strongest supporter. She knows and lives the gospel. She even likes my preaching. The children help me to keep everything in perspective. They are God's richest blessing upon us. They are full of hugs and kisses. Little compares to the importance of being their daddy.

As you look at my family and me, all the church and our neighborhood, you're probably scratching your head in confusion. Everything looks out of place. What are we doing at Southeast? What is Southeast doing at Southeast? What is Southeast doing with us? God does have an unconventional way of doing things. My family and I are White. The Southeast membership is predominantly African-American. Our neighborhood has become about 75 percent Hispanic. We are located in a high crime area, and we don't even have a parking lot. The equation is not exactly a formula for success. No expert would come up with such a design. Our blueprints are not in demand. But there we are, being a church. Our very existence testifies to the hand of God. Only He could create something so foolish and get away with it. We are not something that human genius would contrive. All we can figure is that we must be a sign that the Kingdom is coming, a snapshot of the future for people to see today.

Southeast, like all churches, has revolving doors. We have said good-bye to many who are now in the group shots of other churches in other places. Brother Airdis is a Sunday School superintendent at a small country church in Louisiana. At Southeast he grew from a new Christian to a church leader.

Unfortunately, there are also people that have slipped out the doors without a good story to report. We can only entrust these people to the care of God and ask for mercy where and when we have failed them. It's comforting to know that the Spirit keeps chasing after them, no matter how far from the church they might be.

No, Southeast is not a perfect church. I've only told you what I've wanted you to know. The truth is, we're probably a lot like your church. We're a group of grace-needing people, just trying to serve the Lord and survive in a world that is often against us. There's not a lot of glory—just little signs of the Kingdom's presence that keeps us being a church. It's a good thing that God is merciful.

EXPOSURE 24:

Say "Cheese"

*T*HERE IS ONE SHOT LEFT on this roll of film. The camera is focused on you. Are you a snapshot of the Kingdom? Does your life expose the presence of the future? How about your church? Does your church provide people a glimpse of the Kingdom, a look at the future that God is bringing? That is our task, to live in such a way that the presence of the Kingdom is discernible. Folks who zoom in on us ought to be able to detect that we do not operate under the guidelines of this passing world. Our policies and procedures come from above. We are different. We are, in the words of Peter, "strangers in the world, scattered throughout" (1 Pet. 1:1), or as Paul puts it, "our citizenship is in heaven" (Phil. 3:20). Jesus tells us in John 17:13-16 that we are in the world but not of the world. Just as an accent betrays where one is from, so our living ought to betray the Kingdom to which we belong. More, our living ought to expose what life is like in that Kingdom.

One does not simply decide to go out and be a snapshot of the Kingdom. Such thinking is faulty on two accounts. First, it leads to posing. The Kingdom is not authentically present in a pose. It becomes twisted and hard to detect. Have you ever tried having a four-year-old pose

117

and smile for a picture? They squint their eyes, wrinkle their noses, and pull their lips back, showing as many teeth as they can. The result is a twisted, nearly unrecognizable face that looks more like pain than joy. That's how it is when one merely poses as the Kingdom. The Kingdom becomes nearly unrecognizable. It gets twisted.

Another problem with deciding to be a snapshot of the Kingdom is that such a decision tends to relativize the Kingdom. It betrays that the subject of the picture presumes to have the authority to determine the composition and content of the snapshot. Each change of subject would reveal a different kingdom, suitable to the desires and objectives of that particular subject. There would be as many kingdoms as subjects. The Kingdom would remain unexposed, hidden behind countless lesser kingdoms—and their kings. That is the real fault in deciding to be the Kingdom. The decision presumes we have the authority to define the Kingdom as well as the power to be in the Kingdom. Such a decision reveals that we have not yet come to grips with who is King. We are subjects in the Kingdom, not kings ourselves. Only One is King. Or, in keeping with the metaphor, the Photographer determines the composition and content of each snapshot, not the subjects. The Photographer reveals the Kingdom through His subjects. There is one Kingdom, as there is one Photographer.

So how does one become a snapshot of the Kingdom? Simple. By receiving the Kingdom. Those who demonstrate the presence of the Kingdom are those who have received the Kingdom into their lives. Those who expose the coming future are those who are already receiving it. It makes sense, really. One can't give what one hasn't received. But how does one receive the Kingdom? And what exactly is the Kingdom?

Volumes have been written on the kingdom of God. One of the most comprehensive and yet simplest definitions that I have found is in our daughters' children's

Bible, *The Beginner's Bible.* It states that "God's Kingdom is wherever God is King. And wherever God is King, His love will be found." That pretty much says it all. God's kingdom is the realm in which God is confessed and worshiped and served as King. That realm is ever expanding and ever arriving. One day every knee will bow down before Him, and every tongue will confess that He is King. His kingdom will come in fullness.

Receiving the Kingdom, or entering into it, is not so much a matter of entering into a place, but of entering into a rule, a relationship. To receive the Kingdom is to receive Christ as Lord, as King. It is to surrender oneself to Him. Nothing is withheld—not one's possessions, debts, aspirations, dreams, troubles, pride, relationships, etc. Absolutely everything is surrendered to Him. To seek first the kingdom of God is to give Him complete control of our lives. "Not my will, but yours be done" (Luke 22:42) becomes our deepest prayer, our constant prayer, our only prayer. As we pray and as we obey, God brings His kingdom and establishes His rule within us. We no longer belong to this world; we belong to Him.

A Kingdom relationship with God manifests itself with Kingdom living. Kingdom living is life lived under the directive of the King. The King issues directives primarily by His Spirit through His Word. When the King's instructions are followed and adhered to, the King and His kingdom are revealed. Our living reveals the One who is directing us. As He shapes us and molds us after Christ, we are transformed into reminders of the future. We expose the gospel truth that He is bringing His kingdom. We become snapshots of the Kingdom.

One final thought. We need the Kingdom to come. There is no life—there is no hope—outside the Kingdom. The Church is dead without the presence of the Kingdom. The world is already dead. But we cannot make the Kingdom come. The Kingdom is God's. Only He can bring it; only He can establish it. All we can do is make space for it to come, confessing our need and opening our lives to receive.

Sometimes I think God doesn't bring the Kingdom because we don't have room for it. Our lives are cluttered and full. Perhaps if we emptied ourselves and made room in our lives for God's rule, He would bring the Kingdom in a manner and fullness beyond our wildest imagination. We'll never know unless we give Him space to set up His throne.

Our Father
which art in heaven,
Hallowed be thy name.
Thy kingdom come.
Thy will be done
in earth
[and in me],
as it is in heaven.
Give us this day our daily bread.
And forgive us our debts,
as we forgive our debtors.
And lead us not into temptation,
but deliver us from evil:
For thine is the kingdom,
and the power,
and the glory,
for ever.
Amen.
(Matt. 6:9-13, KJV)